# The $1000 Project

Canna Campbell is a financial planner who runs her own boutique practice, SASS Financial, established in 2006, after a prosperous career in banking.

In 2015, Canna started her YouTube channel, SugarMamma.TV, after realising there was a need to educate, inspire and empower young people around money so that they could realistically build long-term financial freedom for themselves.

# The $1000 Project

## CANNA CAMPBELL

VIKING
*an imprint of*
PENGUIN BOOKS

VIKING

UK | USA | Canada | Ireland | Australia
India | New Zealand | South Africa | China

Penguin Books is part of the Penguin Random House group of companies
whose addresses can be found at global.penguinrandomhouse.com.

Penguin
Random House
Australia

First published by Penguin Random House Australia, 2018

Cover design by Louisa Maggio © Penguin Random House Australia Pty Ltd
Cover photographs: Canna Campbell by Grace Alissa Kyo / Besotted Grace;
polaroid frames by Vitya_M / Shutterstock
Graphs in chapter seven are from *Money Matters* by Peter Thornhill
Typeset by Midland Typesetters, Australia
Colour separation by Splitting Image Colour Studio, Clayton, Victoria
Printed and bound in China

A catalogue record for this
book is available from the
National Library of Australia

NATIONAL
LIBRARY
OF AUSTRALIA

ISBN: 978 0 14378 808 9

penguin.com.au

*This book is dedicated to all the subscribers who have watched me grow, guided me, and allowed me the safety to open up and the strength to share . . .*

# Contents

# CHAPTER ONE

# *The Story Behind the $1000 Project*

## WHAT IS THE $1000 PROJECT?

My passion and determination for showing you how easy it is to manage your own money was what triggered the creation of the $1000 Project.

I really believe that having control over your money is easy – and, more importantly, so many emotional benefits flow from self-discipline in this area of your life. It will give you positive feelings that you deserve to have and carry with you every day of your life, and it only takes a few small changes to create an empowering result.

My background is in financial planning – I talk personal

finances every day. I worked in financial planning part time while I studied at university and after graduating I worked for various financial planning companies, including a major Australian bank, before going out on my own at age 26 to set up my boutique practice, SASS Financial.

I've always been passionate about inspiring people and demonstrating how simple it really is to achieve financial health. But recently I realised that if I wanted to really wake the world up – to ignite excitement and motivation in the dull and overwhelming area of cash flow, budgets and savings – I would have to lead by example. And that meant getting out there and showing people the very powerful effect of small savings that accumulate and compound over the long run.

So I set a very ambitious goal for myself, which I announced on my YouTube channel, SugarMamma.TV. I shared it with my subscribers so that I would feel accountable. I explained that I wanted to build a passive income of $2000 a year, and that I would do that by saving, earning, creating and building parcels of $1000 at a time. Every time I had $1000 saved up, I would invest in some blue-chip Australian shares and international Exchange Traded Funds. These are investments that pay dividends, a form of passive income.

I gave myself a twelve-month deadline, by which point I wanted to have saved and invested enough money so that my investment portfolio was earning $2000 p.a. in passive income. I used an average dividend rate of 5% p.a., the average dividend yield for the Australian share market, which meant I would need to come up with and invest $40 000 – all within twelve months! So the goal I set myself with the $1000 Project was forty 'parcels' of $1000 in one year.

One of the best things about the $1000 Project is that you can start small, work with what you have and work at your own pace and with your own rules – and you control everything. It is simple and easy to follow. And it will teach you a lot about yourself: what you value, what is important to you, and how much strength and determination you really have inside of you. It is empowering. If you get on board with the $1000 Project, I promise you will not regret it.

## WHY WE NEED THE $1000 PROJECT

What is different about this project is that it will finally give you something to show for your hard-earned money.

When you add up how much money you've actually earned so far in your working life, from the moment you started your first full-time job to right now, and see the accumulated dollar amount of your gross salary, most people baulk in horror. The average Australian salary is $75 000 p.a. So if you are 35 years old, you would have earned roughly $1 000 000, assuming that you started work at 21 and averaging that salary out over your working history. When people do their own more accurate calculations, they ask themselves: 'Where has all my money gone?'

This project helps stop that feeling of being clueless and out of control. Next time you ask yourself that question, you will be able to proudly point to a share portfolio that you have built and which is still growing, or to the mortgage that you have paid off, or to the student loans that have evaporated. Or maybe you will simply point to your passport, full of stamps and valuable memories. One thing is for sure: you can choose how you use the $1000 Project to your best financial advantage.

Financial stress can be toxic. Toxic to our health, to our relationships, our careers and our sense of security. But this is an area where we have so much more control than we realise. When we are at peace with money – by which I mean that we feel like we have enough, we feel no negative feelings such as fear, we have trust that it will continue to flow in, we have control over how we choose to spend it, and we use money with respect – the weight comes off our shoulders. This gives us more energy and time to focus on what makes us feel really wealthy: connections to the people around us and living with a sense of purpose and value in the world. I call this 'money mindfulness'.

This isn't a book about materialistic gain. It is about creating financial harmony in your life, so that you are freed up to focus on being the best person you can be. It will help you to know and understand what is important to you and what you value, and then you can choose to live by that.

In dreaming up the $1000 Project, I wanted this challenge to help people learn golden lessons about their finances and their relationship with finances. I really wanted to show people how to save money, how to understand the flow of money, how to be more respectful of their cash flow, and how to make better financial decisions and how to feel proud of their finances. And, as a flow-on effect, I was hoping to educate people about how to consciously use their money in a healthier and more efficient way, which would help them to create a more harmonious financial future.

# *financial stress can be toxic*

Whether you use the $1000 Project to pay off student debt, credit cards or car loans, or to save for a deposit on a home or an investment property, or, perhaps most excitingly, to build a passive income stream – this is life-changing stuff.

## MY PROJECT: HOW I DID IT

### STEP 1: BREAK DOWN GOALS

As a starting point, I looked at how I've achieved my own financial goals in the past. What were the common actions that kept me on track and on schedule? What kept me motivated and feeling like I was heading in the right direction? What kept me focused and passionate so that, when temptation came my way, it deepened my determination and brought me back to the present moment.

I realised it was obvious. When I'd reached previous goals the common denominator was the basic formula of taking a big goal and breaking it down into smaller, more manageable and therefore achievable goals. Small goals that weren't intimidating, scary or unrealistic. They almost felt easy, and this created a sense of excitement and achievement with each little goal kicked – which generated more momentum!

So I set out to build an investment portfolio using parcels of $1000 at a time. Like building a house brick by brick. I took conscious action every time I earned some extra money or saved some money and put it aside so that I could do something great with it.

Head down, bum up, I worked on saving, earning and creating money, focusing on bite-sized amounts. I went to all sorts of lengths to earn and save and then invest that money. But there was one big rule that I set for myself – and this was an important rule – I could not take any money out of my existing salary or savings.

## STEP 2: THIS IS NOT ABOUT SALARY

I really wanted people to realise how important it is to not define yourself or limit yourself by your salary or what you earn. Sure, you may earn a small humble salary, but you also have the opportunity and ability to look, find and create ways to bring wealth into your life, beyond the boundaries of your wage. And to be honest, money has very little to do with what you earn. It's about what you *do* with what you earn.

# it's about what you do with what you earn

Countless times I've heard people say, 'Oh, I can't afford to save, or pay off my debt, or invest. I don't earn enough money . . .' Or, 'Investing is only for wealthy people.' Or, 'When I earn more money, I will think about becoming more financially responsible,' or, 'When I settle down,' or, 'When I am older,' or, 'When I meet the man of my dreams . . .' When people say this, they are holding themselves back from the first steps needed to start great success today. I cannot tell you how many everyday people on humble salaries I have met who have amassed extraordinary wealth. Simple actions and habits, matched with consistency, determination and a commitment to happily living within their means, have enabled them to create a seriously impressive and inspiring pool of wealth and financial independence.

I have also seen plenty of the opposite. I have met people with huge salaries, with close to nothing to show for it, who are in fact living pay cheque to pay cheque. Their lifestyles have only increased with their pay rises and bonuses, and they seem to spend it all before the money has even been deposited into their bank account. They have to keep paddling faster and harder just to keep their heads above water. The stress and pressure on their shoulders is exhausting and ageing. I want you to realise that you are perfectly capable of making additional money. You have skills, items of value, information and knowledge that, if used properly, can be very potent and efficient tools for creating extra money in your life, which can be directed towards building a much more financially secure, stable, consistent and independent future for yourself.

### STEP 3: SET UP FOR SUCCESS

With every goal that we set for ourselves, we need to feel passionately connected to it and excited by it. If we don't get those feelings of deep determination and commitment, the goal can quickly turn into a chore. And chores are easy to put off.

We need to understand our 'why', and our 'why' needs to be the trigger of our positive, enthusiastic 'this will be worth it' attitude. Knowing and understanding our 'why' is what will get us through the tough times, when we feel flat, frustrated and want to throw in the towel. Our 'why' will push us to step up to our next level of ability any time we feel the pull of procrastination or even of quitting.

As soon as I set the goal of a passive income of $2000 p.a. in twelve months' time and connected to my 'why', it triggered so much enthusiasm and excitement within me that I wasted no time. I immediately went into operation mode.

Firstly, I opened a separate online savings account, linked to my personal everyday account, and named it 'The $1000 Project'. Having an online account meant that I didn't have to pay any account-keeping fees, and it was quick and easy to deposit money into it. Plus, being an online savings account, I could earn some interest (albeit a tiny amount). It all adds up!

Nicknaming the account 'The $1000 Project' gave me a stronger sense of purpose, direction and intention. I knew that every dollar deposited into that account was dedicated to my personal challenge. When I checked the account, I could see exactly where I was up to with my goal and how close I was to reaching my $1000 target, and this helped me stay focused and motivated. It also defused the temptation to remove money from the account for anything other than buying more passive income investments.

I'll explain the importance of passive income in more detail later in this book, but broadly speaking, passive income is money that you do not, physically, need to do anything to earn. I like to describe it as like earning money while you sleep. It's your money working for you. Examples of passive income include rent, interest and dividends – my choice was dividends from shares. Because you control the $1000 Project, you can also choose your type of passive income. But more to come about this later.

Every time I deposited money into this account, I wrote in the description box what I'd done to earn it. This helped me when reviewing my progress, as I could see what was working best and what was the most efficient and effective activity to get me closer to my goal.

Then I put together what I call a 'hit list' – I brainstormed as many ways as possible to earn extra money outside of my salary. I bought a notepad and wrote '$1000' forty times in it. Next to each $1000, I listed all the things I could do to create that parcel of money. I wrote down as many different ideas as possible – no idea was too silly or extreme, which allowed me to get creative, and, most importantly, kept me open-minded. Plus, by writing it down, I was putting my goal and desire out into the universe. Seeing it written in black and white, I was bringing it into the physical world, where it could grow into a reality.

I carried that notebook everywhere I went, so that as soon as I came up with an idea, or someone gave me an idea, I wouldn't forget it, even if it was in the middle of the night or if I was in the shower. For those times when for some rare reason I didn't have my trusty notebook with me, I would either send myself a text message with the idea or write it in the notes section of my phone. And as soon as I had my notebook back in my possession, I would add the idea to my list. This meant that all my ideas ended up in one place, so they could be considered, planned and put into action.

As soon as I had enough ideas and activities listed to keep me busy, I set out to work on my first $1000. I put actions behind my intentions, and I ploughed all my energy and focus into coming up with that $1000.

*I was putting my goal and desire out into the universe*

STEP 4: DIVE RIGHT IN!

To get into the project as quickly as possible and to make good headway early into the timeline, I started with the quickest and easiest ideas first. For me, these included selling unwanted clothes, furniture and household items on eBay and Gumtree. Then I did market research jobs where I was paid in cash to talk about my opinion and experience for various products and services – everything from cars to washing detergents . . . I even taste-tested crackers once for $30 cash!

It didn't matter how small the money was, because I knew that every dollar counted. It all meant that I was heading in the right direction towards achieving my ultimate goal.

I also learnt to exercise self-control when it came to spending money. For example, if I had a special event coming up and I needed a new dress, I would either borrow or rent a dress for the evening, and put some of the savings into the $1000 Project account. I actually got a sense of relief not spending money all the time and found it very grounding. It was almost like an act of self-love and preservation, putting this money towards something that would be of great value in my future.

To help create further savings that I could put towards the $1000 Project, I rented my house out on Airbnb for weekends when I was away. I entertained in my own home instead of heading out to restaurants and bars. I learnt to enjoy the peace and nurturing benefits of having quiet and simple weekends at home. I even did a 'Frugal February' challenge, where for one whole month I put myself on a financial fast, only buying the absolute necessities.

The moment I had $1000 sitting in my $1000 Project account, I transferred the money to my share-trading account and purchased $1000 worth of shares. I found that by moving the money out of my account and sending it on its way to getting me closer to my $2000 p.a. passive income goal, I focused my energy on manufacturing the next $1000.

## STEP 5: TRACK PROGRESS

Every time I purchased some shares, I monitored my progress against a percentage system, so that I could see and feel that I was making progress and that all my hard work and dedication was paying off. For example, when I purchased $1000 shares, with an estimated dividend of 5.5% p.a., that meant that I was earning $55 per year in passive dividend income, which was 2.75% of my goal. Yes, that sounds small, but the next time that I bought $1000 worth of shares, with a similar estimated dividend yield, I would be earning $110 p.a. and would be 5.5% of the way to achieving my goal – which is a 100% improvement! Seeing that positive reinforcement is encouraging and gives you a valuable sense of progression.

I would do this every time I knocked another $1000 off my list, slowly getting closer and closer to my goal. And I would review my progress, my next required action and my brainstorming hit list every day: it became a habit that was so automatic and embedded in my head and actions that success began to feel inevitable. Sure, there were times when I ran out of ideas, but I simply returned to doing things that had worked previously.

Every time I came up with $1000, I also shared exactly what I did to create that money, where I invested it and what my percentage was up to on my SugarMamma website and on my YouTube channel. I was hoping that my financial diary would inspire others to join in with me and see how the project could help them get back in control of their financial future.

I also shared what I was doing with my family and friends, so that they could understand what I was passionately working towards. Not only did they give me encouragement and support, but they also contributed suggestions and ideas, and even very occasionally employed me on new paid jobs outside of my ordinary working hours.

## WHAT I LEARNT

There were times where I was in these incredible manifesting zones, with constant flows of ideas and opportunities to create extra cash, and I powered through the parcels of $1000 in quick, efficient bursts. And then, of course, there were periods where the next $1000 was painfully slow, and I would experience immense frustration.

To be perfectly honest, at times I felt exhausted and simply *over it*. But when I felt like that, I would go back to my initial goal and ask myself: How will I feel when I've achieved this? What is my 'why' and why is it important to me? The thought of feeling that pride of achievement was enough to kick any lethargy to the kerb quick smart, and it reinvigorated my self-belief and determination again.

And every time I did something to earn extra money for the $1000 Project, I learnt something about myself and about what I really value. I learnt that having a home-cooked meal over a restaurant meal is better for my soul; that entertaining friends in my home is far more personal and intimate; that saying no and exercising self-control when it comes to shopping gave me greater appreciation of what I already owned. I felt proud of being more selective and conscious of the decisions I made around the way I chose to use money.

## how will I feel when I've achieved this?

I learnt that using my voice to share what I was working on could inspire others, which drove my own energy and motivation.

I learnt that saying no to certain expensive activities sometimes created a sense of relief. I learnt about delayed gratification.

I learnt that I didn't need to outsource as much in my life, and that, with a little bit of organisation and preparation, I am more capable than I realised.

# I am more capable than I realised

I learnt how essential having a foundation of good health and fitness is for maximum energy and inspiration.

I learnt that having a goal to work on increased my sense of self-worth and self-belief. I learnt that saving money is not about depriving yourself but actually showing self-love and respect for your financial health, both now and for the future.

I learnt about the importance of creating memories. I learnt to appreciate the simple things in life again. I learnt about the value of great relationships and connections that actually make us feel wealthy.

I learnt about my own weaknesses and triggers that could sabotage my results – and how to avoid these.

And most importantly, I learnt never to underestimate the power of consciously taking action in small ways to make a big difference.

When I reached my twelve-month deadline, I'd saved and invested $32 000. And I'd built a 100% cash-flow-positive passive income stream of over $1700 p.a. While I was a little short of my ambitious goal, I felt a great sense of pride, as I knew that I'd done the best job I could.

I donated the $1700 to the Gidget Foundation, a charity that supports women going through perinatal anxiety and depression, which is something I struggled with after my son was born. Trying to get out of that scary, dark place was tough, and while I'd recovered before I dreamed up the $1000 Project, it definitely helped me to avoid slipping back into that headspace again. For me, the $1000 Project gave me something to channel my anxious energy towards; it gave me something to shift my focus to; it gave me a sense of direction and purpose; and it helped me believe in myself and my ability to make improvements in my life . . . All these little but important things gave me my self-worth back again.

My plan is to support a different charity every year by donating the passive income that I build.

## YOU CAN DO IT TOO

I'm a self-employed single mother, divorced twice. I had an expensive divorce, with a lot of judgement about it being my second one so early in my life. I have a three-year-old, two dogs that need a lot of exercise and attention and a mortgage, and I live in one of the most expensive cities in the world. At school, I really struggled to keep up with my incredibly bright friends: I had a stutter, and I'm dyslexic and hypersensitive beyond belief. I also enjoy and appreciate a few little luxuries, including champagne, fashion and travel, and, most importantly, spending time with my family and friends.

I juggled all these things while trying to put on a brave face to the world and learning the lessons that I needed to grow wiser. And I did the $1000 Project at the same time.

So if I can get through this and still find ways of creating and saving extra money, and then consciously use that money to build something that gives back to the community, imagine what you could do for yourself!

When I finished the $1000 Project, I took a breather for a few months. I needed some time to recharge and relax. When I announced that I was starting round two, I was blown away by the number of people who watch my YouTube channel who were doing their own versions of the $1000 Project. A lady from New Zealand was preparing for an earlier retirement; a gentleman from the UK wanted passive income from shares; a young beautician running her own business was saving for international holidays; a mother from Sydney wanted to send her children to private school; a lady from Canada was saving money to set up and invest in her herb business, another young couple were doing the $1000 Project to help pay for IVF . . . The emails and stories left me feeling touched and honoured. Some people used the $1000 Project to pay for family holidays – and one couple used it pay for their wedding!

I also received emails and comments from people who had been using the principles of the $1000 Project to pay off credit card debt they'd been carrying for years. They decided enough was enough and the $1000 Project was their catalyst for change and a new financial experience. I even had people tell me that they'd paid off their mortgages using the $1000 Project! Student debt, car loans, personal loans – one women even used the $1000 Project to save for reconstructive surgery that she'd never thought she'd be able to afford. There were also women just like me, rebuilding their lives after a broken relationship: slowly piecing themselves together again and re-emerging from their shells into the light.

And I received notifications and messages from people who had started building share portfolios, and even property port-folios. The project was not only helping people save and get out of debt, it was also helping them to build real, authentic wealth.

Two common themes quickly became apparent. The first was that a lot of these people were describing a new-found pleas-ure and sense of self-respect from being more mindful with their money, which then allowed them to make better, more empow-ering financial decisions. And secondly, people doing the $1000 Project were actually progressing and evolving financially with it. Once people got out of debt using the project's principles, for example, they weren't stopping there. They were taking their new skills to the next level and building up savings and invest-ments and creating passive income for themselves.

The $1000 Project will allow you, too, to consciously pave a path to a much healthier, happier and more fulfilling financial future. It's a journey full of adventure, insight, enlightenment and self-discovery, where financial freedom is very much an achievable goal, well within your reach.

Financial freedom is very much an achievable goal, well within your reach.

# CHAPTER TWO

# *Time to Transform*

When you get started on the $1000 Project, the first thing to do is to set your goals. I believe this is the most valuable stage of the process. Learning how to design and set powerful and meaningful goals will put you on the path to success and give you something to feel proud of and excited about.

## WHY GOAL-SETTING IS SO IMPORTANT

The common denominator with all high achievers is this: they set goals. They aren't complacent, but are always aiming for something better and more rewarding. They have both short-term and long-term goals and the goals are in sync with each other, heading in a positive direction.

When you set meaningful goals – and I mean meaningful to *you* – there is a shift within you. You gain a crystal-clear picture of what you want to achieve, and this drives you. It becomes your purpose, your mission and your vision for the future. So the key at this point is to find out what will spark that excitement within you.

When you're truly committed to your goals, something clicks, and this is when ideas and opportunities open up. You find yourself making different, better decisions, to help turn that picture in your head into a reality.

One of the best things about creating and setting goals is that it gives you insight into what you really value and what makes you happy. It provides a purpose and a target to focus on. And this enables you to channel your energy in positive and constructive directions rather than simply drifting through.

*when you're truly committed to your goals, something clicks*

## FINDING YOUR VALUES

Understanding the essence of what you dream about, love and value helps you create powerful goals that will work for you, and this will make them easier, more enjoyable and more efficient to achieve. The first step is to understand the difference between *society's* goals and *your* goals, because that picture you create must be original and specific to you.

For example, if I set a goal for myself to go to the gym five times a week because I think this is what I *should* do, I'd quickly lose interest, come up with excuses and cut down on my routine. But if I can understand and really keep my focus on something meaningful to me – such as having more energy, feeling fitter, feeling more confident in a swimsuit, seeing my skin and hair glowing, or sleeping better – then I'm going to be a lot more motivated and committed.

And if I get sick, I'll find it easier to be eager and enthusiastic about heading back to the gym the moment I'm well again, and I'll even be excited to rebuild any fitness I might have lost. Having the focus on personal values mean that, when distractions and setbacks happen, they don't stop you dead in your tracks. If you're motivated and focused, it's easier to pick yourself up, brush yourself off, check in with yourself and then refocus on the values you're passionate about and get back on track again, with your eyes on the prize.

Often, when I first meet with clients to discuss their financial plans, they tell me that one of their goals is to buy a house.

Understand

the difference

between

society's

goals and

your goals.

Which, of course, is an admirable goal to have. But sometimes when I ask *why* they want to buy a home, they struggle to answer clearly. They'll say, 'It's time,' or, 'I should,' or, 'It's the logical thing to do.' As we explore further, it often becomes clear that the goal of buying a home isn't really that important to them: rather, it's something that society has told them they should aim for.

If you don't have a strong, connected desire to save up for a home, it won't be something that you pursue with much commitment, determination or passion. And then, even if you achieve that goal, you're unlikely to get that euphoric feeling of accomplishment.

As you set your goals, then, it's important to work out *what* you really want, and *why* you want it. Throw out all you've been told about what you *should* have in order to be happy, and start from this point: what makes your spirit glow with joy and excitement?

# work out what you really want, and why you want it

For some of you, this will be super easy, especially if you're a daydreamer! Your dreams and fantasies can tell you a lot about yourself and what you like, value and want to attract into your life. For others, the answers may not flow initially. That's perfectly normal – and often, in fact, the bigger the block, the bigger the backlog of incredible ideas and inspiration that will pour out once you pull the plug.

To initiate this self-discovery and awakening process, which is the important first step in defining your goals, you need to have a conversation with yourself. Start by asking yourself these questions:

**What do you love doing?**
**What do you dream about?**
**What would make you feel better?**

In the answers to these three questions are your nuggets of gold. And when setbacks happen (as they almost inevitably will), reminding yourself of the values behind your goals is what will give you the strength, passion and dedication to pick yourself up and keep going.

## UNDERSTANDING AND OWNING YOUR GOALS

Here are some financial goals from people I know:

- **Travelling around the world**, particularly to places off the beaten track, learning about amazing cultures, meeting new people and discovering more about myself. Knowing that there is no itinerary and that I can comfortably afford to travel.

- **Enjoying the luxuries of life** – travelling in comfort, exploring interesting countries and cities, while staying at boutique hotels. And being able to do this guilt-free and knowing that I have the complete freedom to do this on my own schedule.
- **Exercising** – going for long walks, especially in the middle of the day when most people are at work, and getting out into the fresh air and simply switching off to enjoy time by myself and feeling the respect of taking care of myself as a priority.
- **Spending time with my pets** – taking my dog to the park, watching him run around excitedly with the other dogs and then collapse in a contented, satisfied heap when we get home. Feeling proud and pleased that I have the time and financial freedom to make my animals a priority in my life, even when expensive vet bills come in.
- **Reading** – immersing myself in a great book, learning more and more about the world and why things happen and what messages and lessons we can take from others' experiences. Feeling proud and secure knowing that I can afford to spend my time as I wish.
- **Adventure** – stepping away from the hectic world and taking myself to the country with wide open spaces and just earth and sky surrounding me. Not feeling the pressure to be at work, meeting deadlines, to get a bonus, to service the mortgage.

- **Playing** with my children, niece and nephews, watching them laugh and play as they grow. Knowing that I can afford to be there for them, and when I am there I'm not worried about budgets and bills and I can give them what they need, while still being grounded.

- **Working on my hobby** – spending time on my blog, knowing that I can afford to work on it full time and have enough freedom to give it the investment that it needs to take it to the next level and let it grow.

- **Laughing with friends**, having deep and unconditional connections with the people who are the rocks of my world. Then being able afford to pay for beautiful food and wine and share this bonding experience in my home or a place that is special to me.

- **Spending time with my family** – being there to pick my children up from school and to make them dinner and read them a book goodnight. Not feeling the demand to be at a desk or climb a corporate ladder.

- **Being there for my significant other** – being able to help them, to share their dreams and goals and to support them. Knowing that I have their back and can be the emotional rock that they need because my finances are secure and stable.

Notice something about this list of goals? They're not actually about wealth and money. These people are looking for strong values in their lives – not dollars. Of course they'll need money to help create these scenarios – but if you look at what they want and personally value, it's freedom, security, peace of mind, comfort, adventure, discoveries and generosity.

When you set your goals, take your time and make sure they're *your* goals, and that you understand the value behind them.

*they're not actually about wealth and money*

If your goal is to buy a house, ask yourself: what would having the house bring you? Security knowing that it belongs to you? Pride knowing that you saved for it? Comfort knowing that you're safe there and can't be moved on? Freedom knowing that it's yours and you can style and decorate it as you wish?

If your goal is to pay off your debts, ask yourself: are you chasing the freedom of knowing that you're debt-free and have no financial responsibility to anyone? Is it the peace of mind of knowing that every dollar you make can be kept for yourself rather than having to use it to pay for things that you've already used or done? Is it the control and responsibility of knowing that you're doing the right thing to prioritise your financial future?

There are no right or wrong answers to these questions: these are your values. You should never second-guess or undermine your values, as understanding them is what will drive you to success.

As mentioned in chapter one, my goal for the $1000 Project was to build a diversified investment portfolio of shares which would produce a passive income of $2000 p.a. My vision was to inspire and educate people to use this way of creating and saving money to help take the financial pressure off their lives.

But, speaking more personally, my ultimate goal is to create a life with no mortgage, a large, diversified investment and superannuation portfolio, and a passive income that covers my living expenses and lifestyle and also allows me to give to the community, charities and people who need a helping hand.

My big picture is to be able to take my family on international holidays every year and travel throughout my own country. I want my family to explore the world together, to see us bonding and working as a team. I want to set a great example and be a role model for my children for when they have their own families. I want to be able to afford healthy and high-quality food, to pay for the education that my children need and want, and of course to know that I can be there for them when they need me and can always help them to the best of my ability. These are the values behind my goal, and this picture is crystal-clear in my mind as I consciously put in place the necessary actions to help get me there.

## HOW TO MAKE YOUR GOALS WORK FOR YOU

### STEP 1: WRITE THEM DOWN

As soon as you know your 'what' (your goals) and your 'why' (your values), you need to write these down. When I do this, I use pen and paper, because that physical connection from my brain to my hand to the pen to the paper inspires a level of creativity and commitment in me. However, you might find it easier writing on your phone, tablet, laptop or desktop – whatever works best for you is fine, as long as it enables you to take ownership of these goals. Also, make sure that you can easily access these written goals, so that you can read them twice a day, morning and night.

One of the most powerful times to read your goals is first thing in the morning when you wake up. It sets your mind on a positive note as you start the day and helps to build your self-confidence. This is also when new, fresh ideas emerge and brainstorming is most effective, which will give you helpful solutions for turning your goals into reality.

Reading your goals before you fall asleep is equally valuable, as you plant powerful instructions into your subconscious mind. This is how you can give your mind permission to come up with creative ideas and solutions to frustrating obstacles and blocks while you sleep.

# know your 'what' (your goals) and your 'why' (your values)

And if you're really motivated, studies have shown that reading your goals before you jump in the shower (or even while you're in the shower) is a great way to trigger new ideas and strategies, because your brain is most relaxed, present and open when you're in the shower. Personally, this is where many of my ideas have been born.

### STEP 2: WATCH YOUR LANGUAGE

Your goals need to be specific and to have deadlines. Don't just have a goal to 'clear credit card debt' – the more information, the better. How much do you need to pay off? Who do you owe the money to? What's the specific date you want to achieve this by?

Your goal would then be written like this: 'Pay off $9000 Visa credit card debt by December 2018.'

Notice the language? First of all, the goal is written as an instruction, so you know you must follow this path without deviation. Secondly, the exact amount you owe and the date by which you want to have it paid off is specified. When you set a goal with a target of 'in three months' time', you often keep pushing the deadline into the future by three months, and it rarely actually gets done. But when you have specific deadline, you're far more accountable and you feel and see the need to put the work in as the date looms.

At all costs, avoid using the words 'no', 'not' and 'don't'! If you have a goal to stop spending money through your credit card, it needs to be solution-based and written in a positive light. For example, your goal could be to 'pay for expenses with cash or debit card only'.

### STEP 3: SORT OUT YOUR PRIORITIES

When you work out your goals, they need to be short-term (i.e. to be achieved within twelve months) and then long-term (i.e. to be achieved in the next ten years). You can set medium-term goals as well, but I've found that as you achieve the short-term goals and keep your focus on the long-term goal, the medium-term goals naturally sprout up on the path towards to the long-term destination.

And two things are essential: your goals must be in sync with each other and you must have your priorities clear. Simultaneous short-term goals to pay off a large credit card debt and to go on a big holiday may work against each other, so you'll need to prioritise one over the other. You have to work on your goals in an efficient manner so that you can keep progressing.

In this case, your goal could be to save up parcels of money to pay off the credit card first and then, once it's paid off completely, you could keep the saving habit up to pay for your holiday. If you really feel the burning desire to have the sensation of working on the second goal, so that it feels real and like you are taking it seriously, then you could open a dedicated saving account for your holiday. That way you don't feel like you're completely neglecting the goal of saving for a holiday, and you've acknowledged and respected the upcoming action required for that goal, while prioritising the debt-reduction goal first.

### STEP 4: KEEP YOURSELF ON TRACK

Once you've written down your goals in the most direct and positive manner, you need to read and review them as often as possible. If you constantly remind yourself of your mission and direction, it will help you to make conscious decisions and to take actions that are aligned to the success of your goals, while reducing or eliminating distractions.

For example, say you set a goal to save a deposit of $50 000 for the purchase of your first home. You may catch yourself in situations that are detrimental to your goal, such as walking around a shopping mall, considering buying items that you don't actually need. But because you're in tune with your goal, you'll be able to quickly identify this negative action and stop or change it.

### STEP 5: GET THROUGH THE TRICKY TIMES

No great goal was ever achieved easily – life is full of temptation, bad luck, accidents and failures. And no one can completely prevent these things from happening. But what will keep you on track to success is the way you handle challenging situations, and your overall attitude.

When tough times happen, you have to try to see the positive, to see that you'll come out wiser, stronger and deeper. Look for the wisdom and lessons in those moments. Grow through the pain, and understand the message, and what you need to learn to become wiser and stronger.

*no great goal was ever achieved easily*

Then come back to your goals, review them, and remind yourself of your values and why they're important to you. Look at what's working and try to make it work even better. See if your goals need to be adjusted so that they feel more realistic. If you need to, break the goals down into even smaller, more manageable goals. Just make sure you're still progressing and heading in the right direction – and feeling good about yourself!

Of course, your values will naturally change as you evolve through life. Always be aware of your values as well as any shifts or changes in your value system, so that you can change your goals accordingly.

As my life has evolved with changes in circumstances – having my son, changes in health – my value system changed.

# grow through the pain, and understand the message

I felt a new awareness within myself of something new that I'd discovered, or that I'd always appreciated but now did so on a deeper level.

You'll know when this happens because when you look at your goals, it will feel like something needs to be added or adjusted for a snugger fit to your unique goals and situation. This is perfectly natural, and in my opinion an incredibly powerful and positive sign, as it shows that you're gaining a deeper insight into and connection with yourself and your amazing capabilities.

So, if you feel in your gut that something needs to be tweaked, don't be afraid to give your goals a little facelift. This will help keep you on track and heading for success. Update your goals by rewriting them, add in more detail from your discovery and continue to read them and put the right actions behind them everyday.

## STEP 6: SHORT-TERM AND LONG-TERM GOALS

As I shared with you, I have a long-term 'big picture' goal, which stemmed originally from a dream. To help get me to my final destination, all my short-term goals are aligned to that final point. So as I accomplish the short-term goals, the success of the long-term goal is almost organic.

For example, say my long-term goal is to build a passive income of $300 000 p.a. All my short-term goals are mini versions of this big goal. This helps me keep pushing myself in the right direction. Always ask yourself, 'What do I need to do to get there?' Each action taken should be positively contributing to achieving your very personal and passionate goal.

The long-term goal for the $1000 Project is for me to eventually make passive income equivalent to the average salary, which is around $75 000 p.a.. However, for each year – as in, my short-term goal – the goal is much smaller, but as each small goal is achieved, it is positively aligned to my long-term dream. I know that if I remain committed to the actions that will achieve the yearly goal, my likelihood of success with the long-term goal is significantly higher.

As you achieve the short-term goals, new ones must be added so that you never fall into the trap of drifting through life or feeling complacent. And always aim for something higher, so that you experience growth beyond the financial side.

Remember, high achievers have goals and success breeds more success, and sometimes it is even contagious, if you're open to it.

Remember, high achievers have goals and success breeds more success.

# CHAPTER THREE

## Your Gentle Guidelines

For the $1000 Project to work, you need some clearly defined rules. Not boring, party-police rules, though – more like encouraging boundaries that will keep you on track, allowing you to get what you've set your head and heart on. You should respect and appreciate them. And this will become increasingly easy to do over time, because you'll see that when you follow these guidelines, and stick to them in the long term, you benefit from the results: not just financially, but in all areas of your life.

What's so great about these guidelines is that they're designed to fit into your real life, allowing you to shape your own approach to the $1000 Project. You shape it around yourself: your personality, spending habits, financial responsibilities, values and activities. The guidelines aren't supposed to be mean or tough, or to deny you any pleasures. Rather, they help give you perspective, balance and appreciation. So they work for you, instead of you working for them.

# what's so great about these guidelines is that they're designed to fit into your real life

These guidelines are what kept me honest, accountable and continuously on the road to achieving my goals for the $1000 Project. They were a serious contributing factor behind me being able to come up with $32 000 over the course of twelve months – something that I definitely wasn't sure I could achieve beforehand.

The rules I created for myself stopped me from wasting my money, from spending it on short-term gratification in the form of snacks, clothes, make-up, shoes – things that I simply didn't need (or need much of) and which wouldn't add value to my life.

Focusing on my guidelines made me realise that most of the time these were just fleeting desires, which, if fulfilled, were quickly replaced by new ones, never giving me the feeling of long-term satisfaction or fulfilment. And they would create more clutter, distraction and unnecessary responsibilities to add to my already overloaded list.

I tried to cheat once – I transferred $50 from my savings account, as a particular $1000 was taking a long time to finish and I was sitting on $950 in my bank account for what felt like an eternity. But I immediately felt guilty, like I had failed myself, and rectified the situation immediately to redeem myself.

Instead of chasing these temporary satisfactions, every time I found savings, learnt to say no or to exercise some self-control, earned extra money from working in the evenings or weekends, or even sold something, I remembered my guidelines and transferred that sum of money into my dedicated savings account. Each time I did this, I was reminded of my bigger-picture goals, which was incredibly beneficial for maintaining my focus, motivation and, most of all, energy.

By having these gentle guidelines working for me, and knowing that they would give my goals the best chance of success, I felt a deep loyalty to them, especially as I'd invented them specifically for my own situation and capabilities. And this felt quite different for me – I have a bit of a self-destructive, rebellious streak, and I usually hate rules! Tell me what to do, and I defiantly go and do the polar opposite. I can't stand being controlled. But give me space and creativity to get things done in my own way and in my own timeframe, and I thrive, not just succeeding but increasing in happiness as well. Allow me to create my own rules and guidelines, with a healthy sense of balance and perspective, and I'll go searching for even more opportunities to generate more success.

By sharing these gentle guidelines with you, and encouraging you to shape your own specific rules to follow in the $1000 Project, I hope to create a similar environment for you to shine with passion and enthusiasm as you work towards your goals. I really believe this is the way to generate the drive to put the necessary actions in place.

## GUIDELINE 1: BE MINDFUL WITH YOUR MONEY

The key difference between most repayments/savings/investment plans and the $1000 Project is that you consciously take money out of your cash flow, beyond your standard earning and spending capabilities, and put it to far better use. This is money earned over and above your normal earnings or salary, money saved by doing extra jobs or adjusting lifestyle habits. You make real savings count, and extra money that you earn is made to really add up. And these two things together are what makes each parcel of $1000 grow as quickly and as easily as possible, so you start achieving your goals sooner and feeling excited about your future again.

We all experience savings and windfalls in our day-to-day lives. Maybe a basic product that you buy every day, such as milk or bread, is on special at your local supermarket, leaving you with more change in your pocket than usual. Or the windfall could be as tiny as finding a $1 coin in the street on your way to work. The key powerful action behind the $1000 Project is that you acknowledge and show gratitude for these financial blessings, big or small, and consciously take them and do something great with them, so they truly count and help you to improve your financial situation.

Let's say you and a friend go out to dinner to your favourite local restaurant, and you expect dinner to cost $50, including a nice glass of wine and maybe even dessert. However, when the bill comes, your friend decides to treat you. Essentially you are saving $50 through your friend's kind generosity. But I guarantee you that by the end of the week, that $50 saving will have evaporated into thin air.

It will have been used to pay for something else (whether in your budget or not), and suddenly you're no longer $50 better off – in fact, you may not even remember where that money went. A $4 coffee here, $10 lunch there, $6 juice, $20 dry-cleaning: even the little things really add up. And before you know it, you need to head back to the ATM, scratching your head and wondering where that $50 went and how it went so quickly – and forgetting all about your friend's kindness and generosity.

However, if you take a second to step back, breathe and appreciate the savings and that moment of relief for your cash flow, then consciously and immediately put that $50 towards achieving your goal, you're being proactive and triggering a powerful shift in your relationship with your personal finances. The act of simply putting that saving from the dinner into a separate and dedicated account can have a big effect. And remember: that dedicated savings account has direction and intention, because it's been set up specifically to help you successfully achieve your goals. Every deposit you make adds up: every single dollar.

This is something that I call 'money mindfulness' – stopping to take the time to acknowledge, appreciate and proactively do something powerful with that financial windfall, respite or saving, no matter how small or big. This gratitude not only helps you financially but also boosts your happiness, sense of harmony and habits.

As you start to use money in this new and more empowering way, it will make you feel in control and like you're heading in the direction of the big picture you've created. And you'll get your first inkling of the potential that exists within you to not only achieve this goal, but other bigger and more exciting goals in your future.

Actively feeling and seeing yourself doing things differently – taking charge in the present moment, making progress and achieving your goals, knowing that they will be accomplished and that you can then set new and even more challenging ones – is what makes the $1000 Project so addictive, driving further growth and results.

Each time you reach your parcel amount, it's like a hit of dopamine. You feel fantastic, in control and proud, and ready

This is something that I call 'money mindfulness' – stopping to take the time to acknowledge, appreciate and proactively do something powerful with that financial windfall, respite or saving, no matter how small or big.

to experience the next breakthrough and see what else you can achieve. You find yourself quickly getting back to work on creating your next $1000. Serious momentum builds, which helps keep you charged and on track for success.

## GUIDELINE 2: WORK WITHIN YOUR REAL LIFE

As I was going through the $1000 Project, I stuck to my existing budget. I did my grocery shopping as usual, I purchased new clothes when I needed to, I socialised with my friends, I still prioritised my health and fitness and, of course, sacred family time. I lived my life as I previously did, and I didn't ever deprive myself.

I did, however, go through my budget and find things that I didn't really need, value or appreciate. For those things, I either reduced them or cut them out completely. When savings were created, I added the savings, no matter how big or small, into the $1000 Project account.

Never did I feel like I was going without – in fact, I learnt to value things so much more. When I did buy new clothes, for example, I found that I got really excited, building up anticipation by working out what I really needed; researching the different shops that I wanted to visit; knowing my budget and sticking to it with respect. Shopping was satisfying again as there were no mindless purchases – and no feelings of guilt. And

I appreciated what I purchased so much more and took greater care with those items so that they'd last longer.

*never did I feel like I was going without – in fact, I learnt to value things so much more*

Catching up with my friends also became more intimate and fun. I prioritised my time by spending it with the people I really care about, and deepening those connections and bonds further. We ended up doing a lot of entertaining in my home and in their homes, which saved all of us money. And having nights with friends in the comfort and warmth of our homes was so much more personal than being in a busy restaurant or bar. We'd all bring something to contribute to the meal – a bottle of wine, a cheese plate and dips, a salad – which evoked feelings of community and family and love.

I spent a lot of simple nights at home with my son, Rocco, curled up on the sofa together, reading books, watching cartoons, doing colouring in on the coffee table, and even cooking. This gave us quality bonding time, just him and me learning more about each other. It cost next to nothing but made me feel rich beyond all measures.

I used the $1000 Project to focus more on the areas of my life that I value the most, rather than depriving myself of pleasure and luxuries. By making my guidelines work within my life, I gained connections, awareness and intimacy – and all the while, the money in my dedicated savings account kept building.

It's the opposite to going on a strict diet, where you throw out everything in your life that gives you pleasure. No carbs, no fat, no animal products, no sugar . . . Sure, for a few days or even a few weeks you may survive. But with such restrictive and aggressive rules, resentment builds, followed by exhaustion and frustration – they don't work within your real life. Then you snap and undo most of your good work and progress as you binge – and then you feel guilty and disappointed in yourself.

The same goes for restriction and control over money. You need a balanced diet, including things that bring you joy (and a few luxuries), matched with sensible and conscious decision-making. If you start from a place of self-love and nurturing, the desire to self-destruct will diminish and results will flourish – and you'll be able to make changes that stick, rather than just setting up something temporary.

*you'll be able to make changes that stick, rather than just setting up something temporary*

## GUIDELINE 3: CONSISTENCY IS KING (OR QUEEN!)

My main rule was that I had to focus on building $1000 at a time, and I had to earn or save this money beyond my salary or existing savings accounts. Every time I earned some extra money outside of my day job, or found a way of saving money through not spending or spending more wisely, I had to immediately deposit that exact amount into my dedicated savings account. It didn't matter if it was $1 or $1000. The rule was that no matter what I did to earn this money, it had to go towards my big goal, my big vision.

Keeping this rule as my consistent focus meant that I was constantly open to and looking for ideas and opportunities, as these new healthy financial habits became part of my life. I found that once I'd incorporated the project into my regular routine, it became second nature for me.

And checking my $1000 Project savings account every day really helped me remained focused on my goal. It was almost like an addiction; I got more and more excited every time I was able to add something to it and see it grow. I left no stone unturned, and the little savings helped to make the big investing happen.

For example, my frequent flyer program was running a special offer, where if I booked and paid for my flights before the end of that week, they would knock $50 off my airfare. I knew that I had to fly interstate for work in the coming months, so by being proactive and booking early, I was able to save $50 – which I immediately transferred into my savings account. Or if I saved on buying lunch during the week by popping home to eat, I would transfer the $10 savings at the end of the day.

Another advantage of being consistently dedicated to this rule – having the money come out of my everyday spending account and consciously relocating it safely into the $1000 Project account – was that I removed temptation completely, along with all the creative excuses that I could come up with to spend it. If it wasn't in my account, I couldn't see it and couldn't spend it.

When people offered me extra work, which I could do over the weekend, I embraced the opportunity. As with the frequent flyer opportunity, when I was emailed loyalty discounts from my local supermarket, I made the most of the savings and transferred the exact amount that I saved from doing my usual weekly shop. When I was invited to participate in market research, I immediately said yes. I knew these were all great opportunities and that even the smallest amount of cash would go straight into the account, taking me closer to that next $1000. Through these consistent, repeated actions, I made every dollar count.

This focus created a strong sense of gratitude for and appreciation of the flow of money for me. I saw how long it takes to earn money, and the lightning speeds at which we spend it. I learnt to savour my hard-earned money and only spend it on things that I loved, valued, used and appreciated. This really raised my energy and headspace and general attitude towards my life and vision.

Following my rules gave me a rush as well, especially each time I actively transferred the next $1000 into my share-trading account and purchased another parcel of shares, after doing my research into which stock I wanted to add to my portfolio. I could see and feel myself getting closer and closer, and I knew that my goal was starting to become my reality. I was building an investment portfolio that paid me a passive income, one that could eventually give me the financial independence of my dreams.

Even though each increase was only a small percentage, I could physically (and mathematically!) see that I was heading in the right direction, and that gave me the encouragement and reassurance to keep going and to know that I was doing the right thing.

*I saw how long it takes to earn money, and the lightning speeds at which we spend it*

## GUIDELINE 4: MAKE YOUR OWN RULES

Your rules for the $1000 Project should be fair and balanced, and they have to come from a good place if they're going to work for you. You need to appreciate them, to see the value and benefit of them. So you need to set rules that will work for you – guidelines that you'll value, respect and adhere to. And yes, maybe some sacrifices will be required, but they'll be *your* sacrifices, which you've chosen for yourself and committed to, and that will make them easier to stick to.

Your rules should help you make your process match your goal. For example, just because I refused to take money out of my salary or existing savings accounts doesn't mean that you need to do the same. You could have a regular amount that comes out of your salary or savings account, or you could kickstart the $1000 Project with savings that you already have. You can find many ways to earn and save extra money. Then, whenever you earn that money or find those savings, you immediately place it in your dedicated savings account, before it evaporates.

The other rule I used, which you could change, is the dollar amount of your parcels – you don't need to work towards $1000 at a time. For me, the amount of $1000 felt achievable and realistic for my earnings, lifestyle and spending habits. I knew that focusing on 'creating' $1000 would be a challenge and a stretch, but still doable and within my reach. And I knew that if I gave this challenge the dedication and commitment that it deserved, it wouldn't take me too long to come up with $1000 at a time, so I wouldn't risk losing momentum and concentration. This is an important factor in working out your parcel size, as you need to see and feel regular, consistent wins on the board to keep you focused.

For some, the amount of $1000 may be overwhelming and even frightening. And that's completely fine – as long as you have a realistic, achevable parcel size to work towards that you genuinely believe you can come up with, you'll be ready to go. Your version of the $1000 Project could be the $500 Project or the $100 Project; it really doesn't matter. This is *your* project.

Of course, some people will find the $1000 amount too easy, meaning they could get bored before they see the benefits. If this is you, make sure you aim for a larger number, a number that's still a stretch, so you can grow both financially and internally from the challenge. Again, this is your challenge, and you set the boundaries.

You can also make the $1000 Project simpler if you need to. You might have a rule, for example, just to make sure that at the end of every day, you put the loose change in your wallet into a money tin or jar. Then, when the container's full, you take it to the bank and put the money towards your goal. You may even want to do this with the notes from your wallet! The point is to make the project's rules work for you – to make them easy to remember and easy to follow, to help you stay on track.

You don't need to set a strict time period, either. If you're someone who finds that 'due dates' suffocate you and make you procrastinate, then you can be flexible with the time limits you set. In my experience, deadlines work. And not just 'in three months' time', but a specific date, so you have a definite point in time that cannot be adjusted or pushed forward. This often triggers the panic that many students experience the night before an assignment is due or before an important exam – and this last-minute panic can be very productive! Deadlines help get stuff done, and on time. They make you accountable.

But if you are making great progress with the $1000 Project and your deadline is coming up, you don't have to stop then, necessarily. These are your rules, so you can change the deadline! If you're in the zone, capitalise on this momentum and focus and push beyond the deadline to see what further progress you can make. If you keep going, this could become part of your everyday routine, and you'll keep the principles of the $1000 Project part of your life indefinitely.

When you look at your goals, look at their size, and look at what you'll need to do to make them a reality. If your goals are very ambitious (good on you!), you should realise that you'll need a significant amount of action, dedication and time. So your timeframe may be a longer one, or you may want to break it down into discrete bursts of time – just like the principle of breaking down a big financial goal into $1000 parcels.

You may wish to adjust or tweak your rules as you go through the $1000 Project. This is not just acceptable, it's great, because it'll mean that you're learning more about yourself and what you value and what you can achieve. Just so long as your adjustments to the rules are not ways of excusing underperformance!

So, give your goal the best rules and framework you can, and the right amount of time and space in your life. Then go for it! You have nothing to lose and so much to gain, even beyond financial wellbeing.

*deadlines help get stuff done, and on time*

# CHAPTER FOUR

## Earn It

The $1000 Project is designed to show you that you're not a victim of your own situation, and that opportunities – even if they're small ones – to find extra money and put it towards something important exist around you all the time. You just need to be open to these ideas, then get up and grab them and don't look back. You'll need to force yourself out of your comfort zone to make it happen, and keep happening, until you achieve your goal.

As you know, in the $1000 Project, there are two ways in which you can manifest your parcels: earning and saving. This chapter focuses on how to earn and create more money in your life. This is your time to hunt, so you must be ready. It's about doing what you need to do to get what you want.

And remember: it's achievable, and while it may not always be easy, it's most definitely worth it.

Sometimes this will mean working as a team with other people in your life, sometimes it will mean working by yourself. Sometimes you'll get up super early, or work late into the night, or over the weekend. You may need to reach out to people you know, or work with new people you haven't met yet, which can be daunting. But as you create each $1000 parcel, you get stronger, smarter and wiser, and you build a thirst to keep going as you see and feel your progress towards your goals. It's exciting and addictive!

Stretching yourself will be so much easier when you have this attitude. It'll give you that much-needed kick up the backside to make the shift, the change, the breakthrough actually happen – which will then pave the way to a much healthier and happier life, with so much more meaning and substance.

*it's about doing what you need to do to get what you want*

## GET CREATIVE!

The first step to earning extra money is to brainstorm as many money-making ideas as possible. No idea is too silly or outrageous; in fact, the crazier the idea, the better. Through opening your mind and imagination, you'll get brilliant light bulb moments. And you'll realise how capable you really are, and that some of your 'crazy' ideas could actually be strokes of genius.

Grab paper and a pen, and brain-dump as many ideas as possible about things you can do to earn or create more cash in your life right now (which you will then deposit into your dedicated $1000 Project savings account). Fill your list with things that you can realistically do today. For example, if you're studying, it's great to know that you'll be able to earn more money when you finish your studies and move into full-time employment, but if you aren't graduating for another year, it's not a solution right now.

Following is a list of ideas for making money that could inspire you. Some of these things are quick and easy, while others require a little bit of planning and preparation. However, they're all reasonable ideas and you should find more than a few that you can do personally – or they might trigger new and interesting ideas of your own.

If you can come up with money-creating ideas that work with your strengths, values and loves, even better. It probably won't even feel like work! I know that when I took on some extra projects on the weekend for cash, I found that I really loved the work and ended up strengthening my knowledge and experience. Look for things that can enrich your life and not only will you benefit financially, but you'll gain other positive outcomes, connections and inspiration.

## MONEY-CREATION IDEAS

- **Sell unwanted items** through eBay, local Facebook groups, Gumtree, garage sales, etc. Free yourself from the clutter in your home and life and make some cold, hard cash at the same time.
- **Dog walk.** This is a great way to get outside in the fresh air and spend more time with animals that get excited when they see you.
- **House-sit.** Instead of paying rent, you earn rent! Plus, you get to explore your city and see what it's like to live in other areas.
- **Babysit.** Spending quality time with kids of all ages is always an eye-opening experience. They may even teach you something! And when I used to babysit on Saturday nights, I found that it was a double saving, as it stopped me going out and spending lots of cash on cabs, food and drinks.
- **Do tutoring.** Helping kids learn, whether it's a language, maths, sport or a musical instrument, is an enriching experience. You're helping to build their confidence and self-worth, and you never know where they may end up thanks to you. I fondly remember all my tutors. (And yes, there were a lot of them, as I always needed a little extra help!)

Look for things that can enrich your life and not only will you benefit financially, but you'll gain other positive outcomes, connections and inspiration.

- **Take on weekend work.** Find a second job that doesn't clash with your normal working hours or study (for example, working in a cafe, restaurant, or at special events). On top of your wages, you may also pull in some good tips!
- **Do photography.** Develop and sell your photography skills – for events, for art, and even for commercial content if you are particularly talented.
- **Rent rooms out to short-term rental companies.** You can rent a room or your whole property – or you can work as a team with someone else to make it a more convenient option. I did this with a friend and we took it in turns renting our homes out: I would stay with him when my place was rented and he would stay at mine when his was rented. Just make sure that your personal belongings are secure, and that you check your guests' reviews carefully before you accept them.
- **Offer experiences to tourists.** Sell certain skills or expertise to people, such as giving tours, pottery lessons, art classes, surfing – the wide range of experiences is amazing.
- **Rent your car out.** This is particularly good if you don't use your car much or if you have a reliable public transport system handy. Again, be sensible and go through a reputable car renting service so that all the necessary checks and insurance are in place.
- **Start a rental business.** If you're passionate about fashion, you could rent out your dresses and handbags to people for special events.

- **Do market research.** I did this a lot and always loved it. You get to talk with people about your experiences of and opinions on different products and services. Hearing people's varying perspectives is always interesting, and you're normally paid in cash at the end of each session.
- **Provide a selling website service.** If you know how to sell on eBay and already have a store set up, you could offer to sell items for other people and charge a fee or commission. There are heaps of people who have wardrobes and garages filled with items they'd love to get rid of, but are too time-poor or don't know how to do it themselves, and would happily pay you to do it for them.
- **Set up a small business.** Obviously, starting any new business has its risks, so make sure you do your research first. Ask for advice from people who have set up a business similar to the one you have in mind. And start small: see what you can do in your spare time before making any major commitment, and learn as much as you can as quickly as possible. Also, do be mindful of any initial lump-sum investment needed to start the business, and how that might affect you financially.
- **Join Airtasker.** The amount of jobs listed on Airtasker by time-poor people is incredible, and some of them are quick and easy, such as moving furniture, putting together flat-pack furniture and painting rooms. All of these are within most people's capabilities.

- **Deliver food.** UberEATs, Foodora or even your local takeaway restaurants – if you have a bike or car, you are good to go!
- **Take on extra projects at work.** Ask to take on additional jobs for which you might be able to earn a bonus, or which will work towards a promotion or pay rise. These things also improve your experience and knowledge, making you more valuable.
- **Ask for a pay rise.** If it's been a while since your last salary review, and your education and experience have increased your value to the company, book in a time for that conversation with your boss. Do your homework into what others in similar roles are being paid, and demonstrate clearly and practically how much you're worth to the business. Worst-case scenario, they say no, and you can use the feedback you receive to keep building your skills and experience and have the conversation again at a later date. Either way, you have nothing to lose – and if you don't ask, it may never happen!
- **Do proofreading work.** Proofreading is great for people who need to be at home, as most of the work can be done online. If you have an eye for detail and excellent grammar and spelling, you may be of great assistance to someone.
- **Get paid to test apps.** Before apps launch into the market, their functionality and user-friendly appeal need to be tested. Apps cost a lot of money to build, so developers really value feedback before taking them to the market.

- **Become an Uber driver.** This isn't for everyone, but I'm a huge fan of Uber and often chat with the drivers about why they decided to become a driver. They all love the extra cash, flexibility and meeting new people. If you have a car that meets the requirements, this is could be a good option for you.
- **Do labouring work.** Love being fit and healthy and outdoors? Labouring work can be a great option if you're happy to get your hands dirty!
- **Start a blog or write for blogs and websites.** Blogs can take a while to monetise, however, so patience and dedication is required. While you build your own, you could approach other websites and offer to write content for them. Even if they can't pay you, some will let you include links to your website, which will help build your traffic faster.
- **Work extra hours.** This is especially helpful if you're a shift worker and can get overtime rates.
- **Make something.** Try anything that can be sold at markets or through online stores like Etsy, such as cakes, homewares, clothes, or arts and crafts. Having a creative outlet is also good for the soul!
- **Get some freelancing work.** If you know how to do graphic design, social or digital media, use Photoshop, build websites, etc., you could pick up freelancing jobs that you can do in your own time at home.
- **Get some temping work.** If you work part-time or are studying, you could make yourself available as a temp to do

relief shifts or help companies when workloads are high. It can pay well, and you can choose which jobs you want to take. Plus, if the employer likes you, you never know what opportunities could open up!

- **Cook.** Sell your culinary skills by making precooked meals for busy people.
- **Wash cars.** Living in the inner city, I can't park near a water outlet, and I definitely can't get a power cord to reach the car to vacuum it. So my option is either to take my car somewhere else or to pay someone to come and clean it. Being time-poor myself – and having a three-year-old and dogs that are in the car every day – I really appreciate it when someone washes and cleans my car. It's a huge help! Do a letterbox drop in areas where this service would be of value to people.

## REACH OUT TO OTHERS

Obviously only you know what you can do, and you do need to work around your existing lifestyle and commitments, but never stop looking for ideas. And remember to share what you're working on with people in your life. You never know who might be able to help you or give you an amazing opportunity or suggestion.

For example, when I began doing market research after work hours, I initially had to turn many offers down, as I needed to look after my son, Rocco, or pay a babysitter, which would use up a lot of the money I earned. But when I mentioned this to my parents, they immediately offered to help me by looking after Rocco for the hour or two necessary – they wanted to support me as I did the $1000 Project. Suddenly, I could accept those market research opportunities.

A similar situation happened to one of my friends, who wanted to do a market stall but didn't think she had enough items to sell. When she mentioned this to three of her friends, they asked to share the stall with her, splitting the cost between them, and it ended up being a very lucrative day for all four people.

I made my friends aware of my personal challenge, and they kept their ears to the ground for me and helped to spread the word that I was looking for extra work. I can't tell you how many golden opportunities came to me this way. When people see you really having a crack at trying to do something challenging, different or brave, they often go out of their way to offer help, support, ideas or opportunities, inspired by your contagious positive attitude and determination.

A young women I spoke to was desperate to pay off her student debt and credit cards as quickly as possible. She wasn't able to earn any extra money from her full-time job, so she decided to house-sit for people in her area and help look after their pets while they were on holiday. She absolutely loved this, as she was being paid cash to live in some amazing homes and enjoyed being around animals. Word got around that she was reliable and loved dogs, so more people approached her to look after their homes and pets. Accepting these opportunities helped her to achieve her goal, and didn't affect her full-time job.

There's something very powerful and inspiring about sharing with others that you're trying to achieve something or are working towards a particular goal, and explaining the reasons behind it. People like seeing others having a go and helping them to succeed.

I saw a classic example of this when I spoke with a woman from Hervey Bay in Queensland, who was worried about not having enough cash to retire. She shared her concerns with her boss, and told him she was looking for ideas to help her come up with more money to put into her superannuation account. Her boss kindly explained that he couldn't increase her hours – but to try and help her out, he offered her work cleaning his house. Through doing this, she discovered that he lived alone and didn't know how to cook – and he was wasting lots of money buying takeaway every night, which wasn't helping his health. So she started cooking him meals while cooking her own dinner at home, and earned even more cash doing so.

Sharing your goals – what you are doing and why – with people in your life may also end up inspiring them to join you and do the $1000 Project for themselves! Then you can keep each other in check, on track and motivated, just like exercise buddies. Energy is contagious, so if you're both excited and inspired, your achievements will multiply.

*energy is contagious, so if you're both excited and inspired, your achievements will multiply*

## KEEP MOVING

As you try to create and earn more money, inevitably you'll be faced with obstacles, but you can't just give up and walk away. You need to keep moving and find ways to overcome or rise above the challenges. I truly believe that when you really want something badly, and you keep trying, you'll find a way to achieve it – or something even better.

Look to work around the brick walls; use them as an opportunity to get smarter and to keep growing. You never know what might be born from trying to think differently to overcome setbacks or challenges.

I remember speaking to a young advertising executive who worked long hours in her full-time job and only had the weekends spare. She wanted to save up a deposit for her first home, so she decided to do the $1000 Project to help achieve her goal sooner. Time was really tight for her, but after brainstorming, and thinking about her own talents and resources, she remembered that she was good at carpentry, and she started making giant Jenga sets and selling them on eBay. The sets were so popular that she was approached to rent them out for parties and special events. Not only was she making some extra cash in her small amount of spare time, but a rental business was also born!

As you progress through your $1000 Project, you need to think about your flow of success. Sometimes, for example, I worked in aggressive bursts of action (particularly when reviewing my progress against a looming deadline!). This would trigger the panic, adrenaline and new ideas, and killed any procrastination. However, you might be someone who works better with a routine or consistency, where you're happy with your steady flow of financial parcels. It doesn't matter at all, as long as it works for you and your situation and goals.

It's important to constantly review your progress, however, and your deadlines. Track what money is coming in, when and from where. Write down exactly what you have earned from different jobs, tasks or projects, and how long they took you. What ideas and activities give you the quickest inflow of money? What's giving you the *easiest* inflow of money? How can you dedicate more time to the project, if necessary? Writing these things down will help give you more clarity on where to focus your energy.

At times, you might need to push yourself out of your comfort zone to accept an opportunity. You may need to be flexible and adaptable to meet a situation, challenge or opportunity; you may even need to put on a brave face and grit your teeth. But if you know something will help you get a step closer to your goal, simply go for it and focus on the feeling of satisfaction, pride and achievement that will come from the hard work. Remember: what doesn't kill you only makes you stronger.

*it's important to constantly review your progress and your deadlines*

Having said that, make sure you're fair to yourself. Don't punish or judge yourself if you genuinely don't want to do a particular job, just because it would mean missing out on some money. The $1000 Project is supposed to be fun and inspiring, and to help build your self-worth, so you need to understand and respect your boundaries. Don't let these moments set you back; just look for other ideas and opportunities that do sit within your value system.

So here's the breakdown for this part of the $1000 Project, as you try as many ideas as possible to earn and create more money:

- Think about your skills and experience, and how you can provide something useful or beneficial to people.
- Consider what resources you can access to help you.
- Think about what you enjoy doing, and whether there's a way to make some money out of it.
- Never underestimate the value that you can provide. Be mindful of and believe in your talents.
- Realise that new ideas will come as you are going through the process, so don't worry about hitting blocks. Often a breakthrough brings with it amazing new ideas and solutions.
- And if you get really stuck in those blocks, simply repeat what worked previously, and make sure to review and celebrate each $1000 so that you can keep your progress on track.

Got it? Then get moving!

# CHAPTER FIVE

# Pennies for Pounds

I never got to meet my paternal great-grandmother, but she used to say to my father, 'Look after the pennies and the pounds will look after themselves.' He passed that little piece of wisdom on to me, and now it's something I try to live by.

How often do you think, *Oh, so what, it's only $X*? Or, *I can't be bothered*, or, *That saving isn't worth my time . . .*? I know I do it more than I like to admit.

With our cashless society – particularly now with options like tap-and-go, payWave, Apple Pay, bitcoin and Mobile Money – we burn through money like there's no tomorrow. Getting into credit card debt is disturbingly easy and fast as we swipe, tap or beep away our hard-earned dollars.

Stepping back to pause, reflect and honestly look at the way we spend money can be incredibly insightful. If we are open to the truth, it can give us a powerful understanding into what we value, what we don't value, and why.

With this deeper understanding of ourselves and our finances, we can then make better and more rewarding purchases, ones that suit us better and give us more fulfilment. And, most importantly, we can reduce or avoid those regretted expensive purchases.

As I mentioned in chapter three, I call this 'money mindfulness'.

For example, we now live in a world where a lot of us (including myself) outsource many things without even thinking about it. House cleaning, gardening, cooking, ironing, maintenance . . . You only need to read the tasks posted on websites such as Airtasker to see how time-poor – or possibly lazy! – we've become. (Again, I wholeheartedly include myself in this!)

Only the other day I was thinking of putting a call out on Airtasker for a handyman or woman to come over and fix a few things around my house that I'd been procrastinating about for way too long. I justified this to myself by thinking I'd kill a few birds with one stone and get some weeding done in my garden while they were here.

Just as I was about to post the task, I stopped – I knew I'd caught myself red-handed. I deleted the ad, and the next day, Rocco and I headed to our local hardware store and purchased the items that we needed to fix everything ourselves. I watched tutorials on YouTube so that I knew what I was doing, and

Look after
the pennies
and the
pounds will
look after
themselves.

I explained to the shop assistant at the hardware store what I was trying to fix so that he could advise me accordingly. Then we successfully fixed everything ourselves!

I actually felt a little embarrassed about how simple these tasks were to complete, and that I'd been prepared to pay someone to do them for me. But I also had a feeling of pride and satisfaction in seeing what I'd accomplished all by myself.

Even the weeding of the garden was enjoyable. It was cathartic, working with nature, seeing the deep, strong roots of the weeds pulled out by my hands – and being covered in dirt felt like fun! I was like a child again and Rocco was in heaven as we cleared space for new herbs to be planted and nurtured. Such a simple thing, but it gave me strong feelings of fulfilment and pleasure.

## GET TO THE HEART OF YOUR SPENDING

If you want to have a go at truly understanding your habits around money, I recommend that for at least thirty days you pay for everything in cash. And every time you buy something, write it down in a diary or notebook. Then review it at the end of the day, the end of the week and the end of the thirty days.

You'll get a shock when you see how those little things add up, and it'll give you a massive wake-up call about how unconscious you are about money and consumption. Paying for things in cash, physically handing the money over and seeing $50 notes break down into smaller and smaller denominations, forces you to stop and question. Are you *really* buying the item because you need it or genuinely want it?

## you'll get a shock when you see how those little things add up

This has been called the 'flinch moment', and was first documented by Drazen Prelec, a professor of economics at MIT. He discovered that paying for items in cold, hard cash causes physical pain. Therefore we avoid paying out as much.

I know people who have done the financial journaling thirty-day exercise and gained such a love for the insight and understanding about themselves that they kept up the journaling beyond the thirty days, and continue to pay for things in cash. They've found it gives them so much more control and helps to form a healthy habit system around money, preventing toxic spending from sliding back into their lives.

I remember going through a short (thank goodness) phase in my life when my designer-clothes shopping got a little out of control. The truth was that I wasn't happy at home, and the respect, warmth and acknowledgment of the lovely shop assistants at my favourite stores, combined with the feeling of putting on a fresh, new, beautiful item of clothing, gave me a short-term fix.

Fortunately, I paid attention to the guilt that I experienced after shopping like this, and spent some time reflecting on and understanding my triggers. I learnt how to manage those feelings in more constructive ways, saving myself time and money.

## DEFINE YOUR VALUE SYSTEM

When I was doing the $1000 Project, even little savings helped me get closer and closer to my goal. Sometimes there were tiny savings that most people would laugh at or not worry about, but to me, they were valuable. They represented progress and contributed to my feeling of momentum. However, everyone has different value systems when it comes to money, and we need to respect each other's. For example, one person may value an expensive membership to a sports club, which some could see as being snobby. But to that individual, being part of that club could represent having a place to disconnect, to recharge their batteries, and to socialise with people with whom they share a common passion.

The same goes for clothes. Some people think of fashion as a shallow pursuit, while others really value the creative process of putting together an outfit, appreciating the workmanship, style and cut, and how the clothes and accessories make them feel in the process of getting 'dressed up'.

It doesn't matter if your value system includes wine, art, cars, clothes, designer handbags (me!), special restaurants or holidays filled with adventure. As long as there is genuine appreciation, mindfulness, gratitude and, most importantly, an understanding of *why* you feel it necessary to spend money on that particular item, service or experience, it's perfectly acceptable.

I feel that if we could sometimes stop and try to understand each other's value systems a little more deeply, with an open mind and heart, we'd have less stress and pressure and fewer arguments about the way we handle money.

While I was doing my $1000 Project, my cleaner (yes, shock horror, I am supposed to be wise and frugal with money but I have a cleaner!) had to stop work due to medical reasons. She offered to help me find someone who could cover her while she focused on her recovery, but I decided to do the household cleaning myself and put the savings towards the $1000 Project.

During that period, I saved $3000, which to me was a lot of money. I became really good at cleaning – I actually became almost neurotic about it! And I made a much bigger effort to try to maintain the cleanliness for as long as possible, after putting my own blood, sweat and tears into scrubbing the bathroom floor.

Over time, though, I realised how much I valued paying for a cleaner. I was missing out on quality time with Rocco while I was furiously pushing the vacuum around his feet, and I was exhausting myself. So, even though I'd saved a small fortune, I re-hired my cleaner and now pay for this service with absolute joy and gratitude. By going through this mindful and reflective process, I gained insight into my own personal value system.

Of course, there needs to be a strong sense of balance, and you have to work out exactly what your priorities are. Be selective, focus on what's really special to you, and make sure you're only spending on things that you love. The fewer there are, the more you will treasure them.

> *be selective, focus on what's really special to you, and make sure you're only spending on things that you love*

## START TO SAVE!

So, as well as finding ways to earn extra money, you can find ways to save money which you can then put towards your

$1000 Project. From little things like taking lunch to work one day a week instead of buying it, to big things like skipping (or maybe downsizing) your annual holiday – there are plenty of ways to help free up extra cash in your life.

Here's a list of ideas to save money that I brainstormed for myself, to help you kick off your own saving ideas.

MONEY-SAVING IDEAS

- **Food plan to save money on groceries.** When you do a budget, food is often one of the biggest expenses. I have a budgeting app called SugarBudget, which is available from the Apple App Store. Planning ahead and thinking through your activities and your weaknesses (e.g. tired = home delivery), can save you a lot of money and also help you eat more healthily. Take ten minutes before you head to the supermarket and plan your meals for the week while cross-checking your diary. For nights when you'll need to work late, or have family activities or sport late in the day, make sure you've got easy meals to cook, or even precooked meals. This saves you time as well as money, as you won't have to go back to the supermarket to get missing ingredients – and we all know that popping into the supermarket to pick up 'just one thing' is nearly impossible. I save money by using Marley Spoon. It is a recipe and meal box service and it costs $70 per week for three meals for two people. Plus the selection is wide and the ingredients are delicious.

- **Have more nights in rather than out.** This was a big saving tip for me. Not that I wine and dine in expensive restaurants all the time, in fact one of my favourite restaurants is a cheap and cheerful Japanese place in the suburbs. But staying in or having people over to mine saved me on babysitting, cabs, restaurants and overpriced wine. Plus we could be as loud as we liked!

- **Research before you head to the stores or shop online.** I've saved myself so much money from doing research before buying things. I read product reviews and recommendations and check prices, special offers and even competitions. Not only do I save money, but I buy products that are better and more suited to what I actually need.

- **Use loyalty programs.** Even small savings from loyalty programs here and there really add up through the year. Participate in them wherever available, and when you see the discount or promotion being applied to your purchase, transfer that amount into your $1000 Project account. I was able to save a large amount of money through airline frequent flyer programs. I used my points to pay for domestic flights and upgrades on international flights, with the savings running into the multiple thousands of dollars.

- **Be mindful of your electricity, gas and petrol usage.** Turn lights off in rooms not being occupied. Put a jumper on before turning the heater on. (I sound like my dad!) Don't drive on the freeway with the windows down – this makes the car less aerodynamic so it burns more petrol. Have shorter showers. All these small lifestyle changes really add up, and they're also better for the environment.

- **Look for quality over quantity.** That cashmere jumper may cost more in the first instance, but it will keep you warmer, be softer and last longer than a polyester one. When it comes to clothes, think of dollar per wear.

- **Change your recreational spending habits.** Don't spend your weekends at shopping malls or your evenings at home on the couch looking at fashion websites. Unsubscribe from all social-media temptation (Instagram, Facebook, mailing lists, etc.) – or keep only a select few that are your absolute favourites.

- **Swap or borrow items with family and friends.** Need a new dress? Maybe your friend could lend you one, or maybe she has her eye on one of your dresses! I've done this plenty of times with close girlfriends and not only do we love thinking that we've got the bargain of a lifetime, we carry a reminder of that special friendship every time we put the item on.

- **Carry a reusable bottle of water.** This will stop you from buying water or juices, and staying hydrated reduces snacking (another saving!). It's also better for the environment to not be buying plastic containers all the time.

- **Invest in a slow cooker and cook in bulk.** My boyfriend, Tom, always says, 'Cook once, eat twice.' Cooking in bulk is cheaper, and making multiple servings means you can either feed more people or freeze some of the meals for nights when you get home late and want a quick, easy, ready-to-go dinner. Plus, slow cookers use less electricity than a light bulb and retain the nutritional value of the food.

- **Catch more public transport, cycle or walk.** No worrying about parking (or parking tickets), petrol or wear and tear on your car.

- **Buy second-hand clothes.** There are so many online shops and groups on Facebook selling second-hand clothes and accessories. I love fashion, and shopping this way has saved me thousands. Some of the items I purchased 'secondhand' still had the tag on and had never been worn.

- **Build a capsule wardrobe.** This is a small collection of clothes that only includes items that you love, that are really versatile, and that can be mixed and matched in a variety of ways. Spend time thinking about your personal style and taste, too, so that you avoid buyer's remorse when it comes to clothes shopping. I have a great video on my YouTube channel on how to build a capsule wardrobe.

- **Utilise your freezer space.** Stop throwing out uneaten food and start making the most of your freezer space. This will also save you money on your electricity bill, as the fuller your freezer is, the less energy it uses.

- **Swap your gym membership for outdoor exercise** such as swimming at the beach or doing circuits in your local park. Just make sure that you maintain your healthy habits! Sometimes when I exercise in the park with Rocco, I carry him and use him as my weight. He loves it.

- **Get on the phone and ask your utilities providers how to get your bills down.** If they're worried that they'll lose you as a loyal paying customer, they may offer you a special discount. Even if it's only for a short period, it all helps! Don't be afraid to ask and negotiate.
- **Make coffee at home.** There's something nice about supporting your local cafes, but the cost of coffee throughout the year adds up. And, if you're like me, you can't get just a coffee – I have to get a muffin or some banana bread while I'm there, so that $4 coffee turns into a $10 excursion. Look at what you value and how many coffees you get outside of the home, and if it adds up, it may be worth investing in a coffee machine.
- **Start a food co-op** through your local markets, shop in bulk for greater discounts and share the produce across your neighbourhood or group of friends. Not only does this create a great community feel, but you're also supporting the farmers directly. Cutting out the middle man means that you save money and the farmer makes enough profit to keep going – and you may also end up with fresher produce.
- **Grow your own herbs.** Herbs cost at least $3 at my local supermarket, and you need much less for cooking than the massive bunch they come in – and they also go off very quickly unless frozen. Having a herb garden at home is a great way to save money and increase the flavours of your meals, plus you can make it organic!

- **Review your home entertainment expenses.** For example, if you have pay TV and you don't want to cancel it completely, maybe see if there's a more cost-effective package that doesn't include the channels that you never watch.

- **Review your mobile phone contract.** Mobile phone and home internet packages are getting more and more competitively priced. Shop around and you may find better offers with your current provider or one of their competitors, providing you with instant savings.

- **Review your interest rates on loans** such as mortgages, car loans and personal loans. There may be a better interest rate or package available, and a reduction of even 0.5% could mean savings of tens of thousands over the life of your loan. Just make sure that if you do refinance, you keep the same length of time of your loan (or even less), rather than extending the debt repayment term.

- **Use shopping apps** such as Shoptagr which let you know when the items on your wish list go on sale.

- **Use coupon apps** that search for unexpired promo codes to add to your shopping cart before you check out.

## MAKE THE SAVINGS COUNT

To make your savings count towards the $1000 Project account, you actually have to be quite organised and proactive when you save money, otherwise those savings can disappear. Every time you create savings from changing your spending habits, or when blessings and unexpected savings fall into your lap, you *must* transfer that amount into your dedicated account.

When I was a child growing up, my family only went to restaurants on special occasions, such as birthdays or Mother's Day. It was something that we got excited about – we'd even get dressed up for something as 'fancy' as our local Chinese restaurant!

These days, a lot of us go to a restaurant once a week – at least. And we don't even give it a thought. It's not for special occasions, but to catch up with friends, or because we simply cannot be bothered to cook or clean up. (Yes, I am also very guilty here.)

When I thought about how this change has affected my own life, I couldn't help but think that I had started to take this luxury for granted. Don't get me wrong, I love going to a restaurant and not having to buy ingredients, cook or clean up – but when did I lose my perspective?

Some of my best memories of meals have nothing to do with the location – they're more about the connection or bond that I was experiencing with the people around me. Hysterical laughing, shoulders to cry on, inspiring stories shared; listening to people, hearing people. Creating moments with people that I love and treasure. I don't need to spend money for any of this.

Now I make a conscious and greater effort to cook meals at home: special meals, where I put care and thought in for the people that I'm preparing the food for. And I try to enjoy the process. Setting the table, switching off all distractions, maybe even having a nice glass of wine . . . I get Rocco involved, too, and we use it as a bonding experience, with the double benefit that not only do we both see it as quality time together, learning new skills and making what I call 'creative happy mess', he is also more enthusiastic about trying new foods if he's cooked them himself (including green vegetables!).

The feeling of gratitude and pride increases the return on the time and effort involved, too (cleaning up time included). That feeling of slowly getting better at something and knowing that you put in an effort rather than paying for effort is valuable and long-lasting.

# FRUGAL FEBRUARY AND MANIFESTING MARCH

While brainstorming ways to manifest my parcels of $1000, I had a light bulb moment – the idea of being a massive tight-arse for a month and seeing what I could save. As it was February, I called this challenge 'Frugal February', and viewed it as a month of financially detoxing or even dieting.

I was excited and also relieved, as I'd been secretly craving a 'right' or 'good enough' reason to say no to elaborate events and unnecessary expenses. And at the end of the month, my bank balance would hopefully be fatter! The $1000 Project was the perfect excuse.

The first time I did Frugal February was insightful. I learnt more about my value system than ever before. Having home-cooked meals, movie nights at home, going for walks in the parks rather than to cafes and bars – I spent more time in nature and with the people I loved. It made me grow as a person.

I also learnt my weaknesses and danger zones, and created distractions and self-discipline strategies to deal with them, like staying off my favourite fashion websites on my phone before going to bed and not going to shopping malls on the weekends. Even little things made a difference, like forcing myself to eat a meal before heading out so I could avoid my usual 'coffee and muffin' pit stop, which was adding up each week.

As usual, I shared my experiences and discoveries on my YouTube channel, and if you watch the videos, you can see that I was riding an emotional roller-coaster.

Frugal February was a process of great self-discovery. However, the second time around was different. A year later, when February was approaching, a subscriber asked via Instagram, 'Will you be doing Frugal February again?' I thought, *Yes, of course!*

Before I knew it, I was in the thick of February and cursing every minute.

It was a different experience. I was angry, frustrated and in a completely wrong and somewhat toxic headspace. I was depriving myself of fun and enjoyable things, and it felt like I was punishing myself. When I did occasionally splash out and get something small for myself, I would beat myself up.

Then I had another light bulb moment. I went back to watch one of my most popular videos, called 'How to Manifest Money'. Now, I know this sounds crazy, but I've always had a spiritual belief about money and how it flows. This is something that I've believed from a young age, and I've seen it play out in many different circumstances, not just for me but for the people around me.

The key is to look at money as energy, and to be open to the flow of money. You respect and appreciate it, particularly when it flows in towards you, and show gratitude to what it helps you create. You need to use your words and thoughts in a positive and considerate manner and stop to appreciate the little inflows of money just as much as the tidal waves.

After watching the video again and understanding why this round of Frugal February was backfiring on me, I decided that after February was finished, I would try 'Manifesting March'.

On the 1st of March, I started applying my own principles, and not only did my attitude and energy go to the next level, I also felt so much happier and more positive about the world and my future. I had a sense of trust, connection and natural, deep appreciation. Even paying my utilities bill was a positive experience.

Within a few weeks, things were shifting. Exciting business opportunities started to flow in, ideas to raise more money for the $1000 Project dropped into my head in the middle of the night – and the opportunity to create this book opened up. Even when negative things happened, like the day I got a parking ticket, I didn't mind, because I was at peace and accepting the flow of money, not just for myself but for others as well. I felt a deeper connection to the world and people around me.

So, if you're going to do the $1000 Project, I encourage you to have a go at both Frugal February and Manifesting March and see what you discover. See what you can learn, how much more aware you can become, and how much you can grow.

# CHAPTER SIX

# The Foundations of Your Financial Future

If you want to build a house – a house that can survive rain, wind, heat and maybe even the odd earthquake – you need to start with strong, solid foundations. That way, when any of these disasters occur, your house will remain standing and any damage won't be too serious. Building financial stability in your life is very similar.

So, what should your top priorities be when it comes to laying the foundations for your personal financial security? Save first? Invest first? Pay off loans first? Figuring it out can be very overwhelming – but the good news is that I'm going to explain it right now!

The goals that you've set for yourself and the $1000 Project will always be your number one focus, of course. Having goals that matter to you and that give you purpose and direction is essential to your happiness and energy for this journey, as I've said before. However, as a licensed financial planner, I feel that it's my responsibility to give you some valuable insight and education into the best ways to use the $1000 Project to create long-term financial freedom. This way, you'll be able to make an educated decision about what's best for you and your future, and you'll feel even more in control and in tune with your vision.

When you realise how helpful these suggestions could be for you and the ways in which they could increase your financial wellbeing, you may want to add some of them to your list of goals. I want you to be aware of all the great things you can achieve from the $1000 Project, so that you can pick and choose what works for you, your needs, your values and your motivation.

I really believe that the first and most important step is to reduce or even completely wipe out toxic debt in your life. Toxic debt is debt that doesn't provide you with any tax deductions, passive income or growth. You can build up this type of debt with, for example, credit cards, car loans, personal loans, student loans (to be explained) and home loans.

Healthy debt, on the other hand, is money that you borrow to do beneficial things, such as to purchase shares, investment properties, businesses or managed funds. These are things that help build your wealth over the long term, providing you with passive income streams and/or capital growth opportunities, as well as some tax deductions along the way.

Generally speaking, if you borrow money to purchase something that generates an income, such as an investment property which you rent out, you can claim the cost of borrowing the money (i.e. the interest) off the income that you receive.

Debt most definitely has its place in our society, and rightly so – without it we wouldn't be able to buy things like homes and investments. But the issue is the amount of debt, what it's used for, and how strongly you focus on actually paying it off.

Ideally, you want no toxic debt and some healthy debt. So, if you're wondering how to get the best financial benefit from doing the $1000 Project and you have toxic debt, a good goal would be to reduce your debt to a more manageable level, or even to pay it off for good.

It can be hard to know what your priorities should be in debt reduction, though. With this in mind, I'm going to outline the different types of debt, from the worst to the least worst, and explain why each is bad and why you need to pay it off. And, most importantly, I'll look at how realistic it is to pay debt off quickly if you put your mind to it. Once you've managed to move off the debt repayment treadmill, you can turn your mind to creating more wealth and stability for yourself!

## PRIORITY 1: CREDIT CARD DEBT

The worst type of debt to have is credit card debt, when you owe money on a credit card that is never or rarely paid off in

The first and
most important
step is to reduce
or even completely
wipe out toxic debt
in your life.

full when it's due. It has the highest interest rate charge (of up to 22% p.a.), and it's damaging to your credit rating – and to your headspace.

*once you've managed to move off the debt repayment treadmill, you can turn your mind to creating more wealth and stability for yourself!*

Your credit rating is a number that tells financial institutions how reliable you are with money, particularly borrowing money (kind of like a report card from school). If you have credit card debt, or even worse, multiple credit card debts, it will negatively affect your credit rating. The lower your credit rating, the harder it will be to borrow money, which could damage your ability to achieve major life goals such as one day buying a home, starting up a new business or investing.

You can find your credit rating relatively easily and quickly online for free. There are plenty of websites that do this for you, but you need to be careful that they don't sell your information on. I recommend sticking to one of the three credit reporting bodies in Australia. If you discover that your rating is low, don't despair: you can rebuild it by taking control of your debt and paying it off as quickly as possible, and by monitoring the amount of credit that you draw on and have access to.

Even if you're paying an interest rate much lower than 22% p.a., this interest is still not tax deductible, and it definitely doesn't provide you with any passive income or with capital growth. Most people who carry this kind of debt don't have much to show for it.

Say that you have $10 000 owing on your credit card and the card has a special interest rate of 12% p.a. Each year, you're wasting over $1200 in interest, which you have to pay with your after-tax earnings. So, depending on your marginal tax rate, you may have to earn $2000 before tax before you can afford to service the interest – and you still haven't paid off any of the principal loan.

The other reason why credit card debt is so bad, beyond the excessive interest rate cost, is that it affects your attitude. Often when I coach people out of debt, they have to get past huge amounts of negative emotions such as guilt, remorse, embarrassment, shame, even disgust. Carrying around these feelings every day isn't good for you or your mental health. And when you're in this kind of debt, it's common to have the disheartened, self-destructive view of, 'Well, I'm already in debt, what does it matter if I buy this dress, laptop, holiday . . .?' Then up goes the debt again. It can become so overwhelming and self-perpetuating that you don't even know where to start to get back in control again.

*you can use the $1000 Project to help you get out of debt*

It's really easy and fast to rack up credit card debt. You might buy a $500 item on a credit card and not give it much thought – but that $500, after tax, might have taken you a couple of days to earn. Yet you spent it so quickly and without much consideration.

The process of using a credit card is a reasonably mindless activity, and so your value system often isn't switched on. As I mentioned in chapter five, the swiping or tapping of a card doesn't make as much impact on you as paying for things in cash, where you feel the full experience of giving away your money. The latter makes you a lot more alert to whether you really value what you're buying, and what you're giving up.

If you're drowning in debt, it doesn't have to be this way. You can use the $1000 Project to help you get out of debt, with each parcel of $1000 that you can throw at it.

And, to be brutally honest, the longer it takes for you to get out of this type of debt, the bigger the lesson that you needed to learn – and, hopefully, the less likely it will be that you'll return to using a credit card so flippantly. Having to go through this big change will create a conscious shift and give you a new appreciation for using money in a more mindful manner.

This is why I'm a little hesitant to recommend that people take out a personal loan to consolidate credit card debt, unless some internal work has been done to stop the excessive use of a credit card and bad habits have been put to rest. Time and time again, I have seen people take out a loan to pay off a painful debt that they've been carrying for a while, with the best intention of sticking to their repayment plan, only to find themselves soon using a credit card again. Then, twelve months later, the total debt has doubled.

If you're using credit cards mindlessly or thoughtlessly, or as an emotional Band-Aid, please take the time while doing the $1000 Project to tackle and break this habit. It'll be extra helpful if you can gain insight into *why* you do this. What are the triggers to watch out for, and what solutions or strategies do you need to empower yourself to move toward a more positive headspace?

So, if you want to use the $1000 Project to rebuild your financial future, start with paying down your credit card debt, and make a lifetime promise to yourself that you will watch what you spend and pay off your card in full every month – or that you will not have a card and will only pay for things in cash.

Sometimes, after paying off stressful amounts of credit card debt, people find that they would much prefer never to have the temptation of a credit card in their possession. They realise that they're financially and mentally better off only paying for things in cash or with their debit card. This leaves them more conscious of their budget and cash flow, as they know they have to make their money last until the end of their pay cycle.

If you are one of these people, have a think about setting a goal to get out of credit card dependency as soon as possible. Learn from your old bad habits and promise yourself that this spending behaviour will die a quick death. You can replace it with a wiser and more empowered practice.

## PRIORITY 2: PERSONAL LOANS AND CAR LOANS

Personal and car loans can be just as toxic as credit card debt, but the interest rate is usually lower, which is why I've rated them second in my list of suggested priorities.

Make a lifetime promise to yourself that you will watch what you spend and pay off your card in full every month – or that you will not have a card and will only pay for things in cash.

Typically, these types of loans are taken out to help consolidate credit card debt, or to pay for a lifestyle asset such as a car or a holiday or other depreciating assets. Either way they still tick all three boxes for a toxic debt label: high interest rates, a negative impact on your ability to borrow money until the debt is paid off, and harmful to your financial attitude. (Occasionally you can claim some of the interest from a car loan, but only for travel for work.)

And, as with credit cards, these types of loan mean that you're paying (plus more with the interest) for something that you purchased ages ago and might not even be still enjoying. With an expensive holiday, for example, the effect of it will fade in your memory while the financial pain and cash flow drag continues on.

If you have this kind of debt, you can use the $1000 Project to clear it sooner and save on interest. This will clear the path for you to move on to other, more positive areas in your finances, and those monthly repayments will stay in your pocket to spend as you wish.

Say that you have a car loan of $30 000, with an interest rate of 14% p.a. on a five-year term. Your monthly repayments would be just under $700 per month. If you can come up with even three parcels of $1000 each year to pay towards the loan, you could have your loan paid off more than a year and a half sooner, saving over $4000 in interest.

So if you have a personal loan or car loan, it's definitely worth considering paying this off as one of your goals for the $1000 Project.

## PRIORITY 3: STUDENT LOANS AND HECS-HELP DEBT

If you never spend a second thinking about, let alone worrying about, your HECS-HELP debt or student loans, I wouldn't blame you in the slightest. These loans are automatically approved, you rarely get an update as to how much you owe and how long it will take to be paid off, and the loan appears to be interest-free. So having a complacent attitude is only natural. And investing in your education (even via a loan) is one of the best investments you can make, as it increases your value and your purpose in the world.

However, it's not all good news for this kind of debt . . . Firstly, these loans are indexed. This means that if you have a student loan debt of $30 000 and the nominal inflation rate of 3% is applied, then the loan will grow by $900 after twelve months. So you need to spend $900 of your after-tax earnings every year just to stop that debt from getting any bigger. And as you probably already know, the bigger the debt, the more challenging it is to pay off.

Secondly, if you earn over a certain amount (currently a little over $55 000 p.a.), your employer will automatically be taking repayments out of your pay as per the Australian Taxation Office's instructions. But as the compulsory repayment rate is between 4 and 8% of your pay, depending on your salary, it will take the average person ten years to pay off their HECS-HELP debt.

Ten years is a long time to be held back financially. Throwing parcels of $1000 towards your HECS debt (ideally before 1 June every year, which is when they apply the index) will dramatically speed up the extinguishing of this debt.

Also, your student debt or HECS debt counts towards that credit score that we were previously talking about. Having large amounts of student debt can reduce the amount of money that you'll be able to borrow.

And finally, while the indexation rate on these types of loans is very low, it is possible that the government will increase it to a more appropriate market rate. The government's attitude has certainly changed over the last couple of years, to the point where they're now even chasing people who have moved overseas to make repayments on their HECS-HELP debt. This indicates things could get stricter some time in the not-so-distant future.

If you have this type of debt, do the work to find out exactly how much you have and put the right actions in place so that you can use your parcels of $1000 to pay it off for good. And when it's gone, enjoy the fact that you have proudly returned the money to the government so that other students can take their turn building their education and career opportunities.

## PRIORITY 4: HOME LOANS

Okay, I'll go a bit easier on home loans. But not too much! Your home – as in the place that you live in, not somewhere you rent out for passive income purposes – carries a lesser form of toxic debt. The reason why I'm a little kinder towards this type of debt is that when these loans require principal and interest repayments, you're forced (ever so slowly) to pay the loan down over time.

Plus, if you're fortunate enough to buy in the right area at the right time, the property may go up in value. However, I say this with caution, as any growth of the property is in relation to other properties in your area. The growth can be beneficial for you, but if you're selling and buying back in the same market, you may end up simply shifting from one expensive asset to another. And in the meantime, the interest adds up to a disturbing amount of money over the long term, which often exceeds the perceived capital growth on your property. And you're holding a large asset that provides no passive income.

So, if you have a home loan, and want to come out as far ahead as possible, one of the smartest things you can do is pay it off as quickly as possible. Having a thirty-year loan and only ever paying the minimum is wasting valuable time and money on interest.

Say you have a home loan of $400 000 with an average interest rate of 6% p.a., and that you pay the minimum monthly repayment that most banks automatically put you on. You've only just purchased this house, so the loan has only just begun. You have thirty years until you own the property outright.

In this scenario, you will pay to the bank over $510 000 in interest over the life of the loan. And that's assuming that you never extend your loan to do renovations, or refinance or redraw any money off the loan.

Also, that $510 000 is money paid with after-tax earnings. So you'll have to earn at least $750 000 or more (depending on your marginal tax rate) to cover that expense.

However, if you were to pay an extra $1000 every two months (roughly $125 per week), adding an extra $6000 p.a. to reducing the loan, starting today and continuing on for the life of the loan, you'd save over $205 000 in interest and pay off the home loan in full 10.5 years sooner.

That $205 000 you've saved can go towards far more exciting things in your life: holidays, helping family members, reducing your working hours, or even an earlier retirement. The choice and freedom is yours. And your monthly cash flow is freed up, as you no longer have to pay $2500 per month in mortgage repayments plus the $500 per month in interest. So you'll have a spare $3000 per month to use to your heart's content – whether it be to spend, to save, to invest or even to give away.

There is also a huge emotional and mental benefit to paying off your mortgage sooner. You'll feel the sense of security that comes from knowing that the bank can't take away your home (assuming no other loans are secured against it). You'll also feel a sense of confidence even if the property market dips, as the reduced value of your home doesn't jeopardise your finances. You'll have comfort in knowing that you have the choice to use the equity in the property, should you wish, as well as general peace of mind. All of which will contribute to a good night's sleep and possibly slow the ageing process!

So, if you like the sound of paying your home off sooner, and not wasting such a huge amount of your hard-earned money over the years, this is definitely something that you could include as one of your goals for the $1000 Project.

*there is also a huge emotional and mental benefit to paying off your mortgage sooner*

## PRIORITY 5: SAVINGS

Having a certain amount of money in savings can give you a valuable sense of security. It can also stop you from reaching for a credit card or a loan in the event of an emergency, big or small: parking fines, unexpected dental work, car repairs, medical emergencies, redundancies, illnesses, and so on. If you've just finished all the hard work of paying off previous debt, you don't want to open the door for bad habits to creep back in.

Unfortunate and costly things can happen suddenly to all of us – they're just a part of life that we have to accept. But we can choose to be well prepared for these obstacles, emergencies and challenges, and I want to help you achieve that. Having a nice amount of money in savings to help defuse stress in your life is a sensible goal to have.

Your first question is likely, 'How much I should have in emergency savings?' If you google this, you'll find all sorts of answers, ranging from several months' worth of salary, to a certain multiple of weekly expenses, to flat dollar amounts.

In my opinion, the only right answer is what will work for you. Young people with a secure job, no debt, family and friends nearby and minimal financial responsibilities may only need a small amount of money for comfort and security. Additional savings beyond this may be a waste of resources for such a person, as that money could be put to better use.

By comparison, a young family relying on one income, with large financial responsibilities and growing family expenses, might prefer a larger amount for peace of mind. They may, for example, want six months' worth of expenses in cash that can be accessed at all times, or $5000 for last-minute flights to see elderly family in an emergency, or simply the security of a specific dollar amount.

Only you can work this out, as the answer revolves around your life and your needs.

Take the time to work out what possible challenges exist in your world and how much money you would need to rectify these problems to the best of your ability. Then make it your goal to use the $1000 Project to build up these necessary savings.

*we can choose to be well prepared for obstacles, emergencies and challenges*

## PRIORITY 6: WEALTH CREATION

If you're toxic-debt free and have built a comfortable nest egg that will cover you for a rainy day, and now you want to think about being completely financially free to choose how to spend your time and where – well then, this is your stop!

The best place to start is to figure out how much money you need to live the life that you desire. Which means knowing how much you spend today, and then adjusting that according to what you really want and need.

Start by writing down all of your living expenses and adding them up to see what the total is. Every single detail has to be considered – from morning coffees and chewing gum to annual holidays and gifts. Leave nothing out, and keep in mind that the more honest you are, the more awareness and understanding of yourself you'll gain.

To help you with this process and to make sure you don't miss any expenses, you could either keep a spending diary for a month, or check your bank and credit card statements carefully – or even better, do both! I actually designed a budgeting app called SugarBudget to help make this as easy as possible for you, and to make it easy to review and update your budget at all times. You can find this in the Apple app store. It even gives you banking instructions to help you achieve your financial goals and reminds you when large quarterly or biannual bills are due, so there are no nasty surprises and you have the cash properly set aside, ready to pay these bills (snagging your money stress-free).

This process of checking your true cost of living is enlightening, but it can also be painfully grounding.

It's human nature in a consumer-driven world to downplay the true extent of our living expenses. When I'm working with financial planning clients, it's so common for me to hear, 'Well, I don't actually spend that much . . .' But then, when we sit down together and go through this process, the colour quickly drains from their faces as the 'calculate total' button is pressed!

I'm guilty of this kind of thinking myself sometimes. But I know that, at the end of the day, living with my head buried in the sand is only doing a massive disservice to myself and to the potential changes and outcomes I can create. So when I check my budget, my savings accounts, my investments, my home loans, my superannuation accounts, they tell the truth. The truth that I need to hear. And from this knowledge comes the motivation for action.

After you've worked out your current living expenses, you then need to add or remove the expenses that you want to include in your goal of being financially free. For example, if you want more holidays, add in enough money to your annual budget to cover that cost. If you want to pay school fees for your children or grandchildren, add them in. If you want to be able to give more to charity, add that in. This is a creative process and you are planting valuable seeds into some seriously fertile soil, so give yourself the freedom to imagine your ideal future.

And remember that your idea of being financially free may not require any more money than what you're currently spending. You might already be happy with your lifestyle – or your goal could actually require less money. For example, you could have a dream of relocating to a small town where the cost of living is much lower, or even to another country where the taxes are less.

When you've established the magic number – your projected annual cost of living – you need to get started buying and building passive income streams so that eventually your passive income can pay for the dream to become your reality.

If you think, for example, your cost of living will be $50 000 p.a. (just under $1000 per week), remember to round this up for tax and add a buffer for emergencies. This means you need to acquire and invest in passive income streams over time that will generate a gross income of $70 000 p.a. for you.

As soon as you know your total magic number, make it one of your key financial goals to start building it as soon as possible. Watch it grow, add to it, reinvest in it and review it regularly so that every step gets you closer and closer, and you can enjoy the pride of knowing that you're really doing this!

This process of checking your true cost of living is enlightening, but it can also be painfully grounding.

# CHAPTER SEVEN

## Sharing Shares

### WHY PASSIVE INCOME?

One of my biggest missions in life is to show people the value
of passive income and how much freedom, independence and
choice it can give you, particularly when that passive income
keeps growing year after year.

As you know, you can use the $1000 Project to create and
build your own passive income supply – if you're ready to. And
having a passive income – allowing your money to work for you,
rather than you working for money – appeals to a lot of people
on a deep level.

I'm absolutely passionate about my job, and honestly don't
ever get Mondayitis or feel that my work is a monotonous

grind. I love the idea of going to work because I choose to, not because I have to. It makes a massive difference to your head-space and attitude when you know that you're not working to pay the bills, but to build something powerful that will benefit your future and the future of others. That feeling of purpose is so important.

So, building naturally growing passive income is a big part of my personal financial goals in life. I don't necessarily intend to retire early (I'm way too hyperactive for early retirement!), but I love the idea of having the freedom to decide how I spend my time, and where.

Passive income offers the freedom to work when I want and where I want. Freedom to say yes to my family when they need me. Freedom to take family holidays where and when I want them. Freedom to experience what I want to. Freedom to give unconditionally to charities or help people in need. Freedom to buy the best food and health care for my family, and freedom to leave situations that don't work for me or my value system.

The main way I'm building my passive income from the $1000 Project is by investing in shares – specifically Australian industrial shares, listed investment companies and some international exchange traded funds. (I'll explain what these are shortly.) These types of investments suit my long-term goals for building passive income and capital growth oppor-tunities, and I understand and accept their high levels of volatility because history shows it'll be worth it for great long-term performance.

Where and how you invest is your decision, and you need to understand the risks, benefits and value of investing to you and your goals. I chose to use the $1000 Project to create greater financial security outside of my salary and savings. I wanted to be proactive in creating something to help take care of me financially and give me the freedom and peace of mind I desire.

## WHAT ARE SHARES?

In my experience, a lot of people are misinformed about investing in shares, and are almost scared of them. If you don't understand how they work, you won't be able to grasp how amazing and beneficial they can be in helping you grow your financial wealth and create more financial harmony in your world.

So in this chapter, I'd like to shine some light on shares so that you can see they aren't really that scary, and maybe you'll realise that they could suit you and your goals. I also want to help you realise that managing your money and building an investment portfolio isn't that hard, especially when you use managed funds, exchange traded funds or listed investment companies. It's a lot simpler than you think.

To start off, you need to understand the very basics. When you own shares in a company, you own part of a business and are referred to as a 'shareholder'. Your ownership is documented electronically or on paper, in exactly the same way that your ownership of real estate would be documented through a title deed.

Many people claim that shares are just bits of paper or 'intangible assets', unlike property – but understand that the businesses you invest in and partly own are just as tangible as a house or flat. The supermarket that I own in my share portfolio – and shop at! – is tangible. The airline that I own in my portfolio – and fly with! – is tangible.

And shares can be incredibly valuable when they're selected carefully in light of your goals, your risk appetite and your financial strategy. You buy shares with the expectation that the business will continue to develop its products and services, which should increase the value of its shares (and your investment). This is known as 'capital growth'.

> *shares can be incredibly valuable when they're selected carefully in light of your goals*

Some of the profits that the business makes each year or half-year are reinvested into the company so that it can continue to grow and produce better and more successful goods and services.

However, many companies will also pay you, a shareholder, some of those profits via 'dividends', which are normally paid twice per year.

This is a form of passive income – similar to the rent you receive for an investment property, but with sweeter benefits.

Keeping things simple, there are three major groupings in our sharemarket in Australia that you should be aware of – the Industrials Index, the Resources Index and the All Ordinaries Index. (An 'index' is a way to measure the share prices of groups of companies – like a thermometer used to monitor the general health of the stocks in that group.)

- **The Industrials Index** contains businesses that make goods and services – companies that we see and deal with on a regular basis, such as supermarkets, airlines, food manufacturers, even transport companies. Essentially, they improve our standard of living.
- **The Resources Index** comprises companies involved in the exploration and mining of minerals, oils and gases. We tend to sell the unprocessed forms of these resources overseas and buy back the finished products.
- **The All Ordinaries Index**, commonly called the 'All Ords', is a measure of the overall performance of the Australian sharemarket. It's an index of the share prices of the largest 500 or so companies in the country.

## Chart 1

**Price Indices**
**Value of $100 000 invested December 1979–2016**

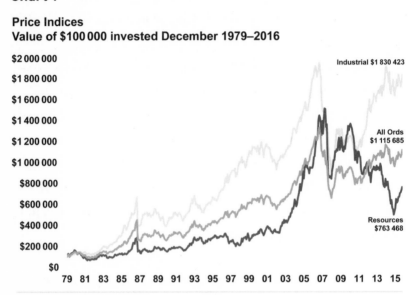

Data: S&P/ASX 200 Industrials Index (All Industrials Index used prior to May 1992).
S&P/ASX 200 Resources Index (All Resources Index used prior to May 1992).
S&P/ASX 200 All Ordinaries Index (All Ordinaries Index used prior to May 1992).

If you refer to the chart above, you can see how much $100 000 invested in each of these three groups in December 1979 would be worth today. Your resources portfolio would be valued at just over $763 000, your All Ords portfolio would be worth just over $1 115 000 – and impressively, your industrials portfolio would be worth over $1 830 000. And that's assuming that you spent all the dividends you received.

Looking at these numbers, I'm sure that you'd have preferred not to have bothered with the All Ords or Resources indexes in 1979, and instead to have put your full $300 000 into industrial shares. A far more efficient and effective application of your funds, don't you think?

Coming back to the conversation around passive income, dividends can be an important part of the $1000 Project journey, if you feel that investing to create passive income sources is going to be your immediate or eventual strategy. Dividends have actually been a bit of a dark horse of the Australian sharemarket, but have contributed impressively towards the total return of the market over time. Take a look at the next chart, which factors in the power of dividends over the long run.

It's the same as the first chart, showing the $100 000 investment into each of the three indexes – but it shows the result the investments would have achieved if the dividends were reinvested

## Chart 2

**Accumulation Indices**
**Value of $100 000 invested December 1979–2016**

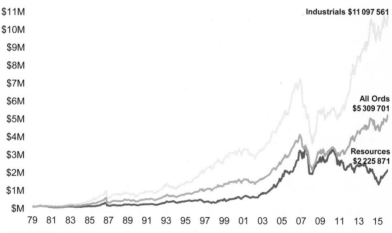

Data:
S&P/ASX 200 Industrials Accumulation Index (All Industrials Accumulation Index used prior to May 1992).
S&P/ASX 200 Resources Accumulation Index (All Resources Accumulation Index used prior to May 1992).
S&P/ASX 200 All Ordinaries Accumulation Index (All Ordinaries Accumulation Index used prior to May 1992).

into the portfolio instead of being spent. Let's just say the term 'blowout' is appropriate – and probably an understatement!

Looking at the chart, you can see the Resources Index is up to an impressive $2 225 000, and the All Ords is even better – worth over $5 309 000. And the Industrials Index is worth over $11 000 000!

Yes, look at the chart again . . . you aren't going cross-eyed. Your industrials portfolio purchased at $100 000 would be worth over 108 times your initial investment. How can that be? $100 000 into $11 000 000 over thirty-seven years?

Well, the answer lies in the fact that shares are two-dimensional, in that they pay income as well as increasing in value. This means that you get a growing passive (dividend) income over time, because the value of the asset increases over time. A $3 stock paying a 15¢ dividend becomes, thirty years later, a $24 stock paying a $1.40 dividend – your last dividend payment could end up being more than 46.5% of your initial investment!

The dividends grow with the value of the asset, which is really powerful when you allow time to let your portfolio grow in value. As an extra bonus, industrial shares often come with tax credits, which I will explain shortly.

Now, some people will say that shares are volatile, but their dividends are actually considered to be less volatile. Without getting too complicated (and possibly boring), the worst annual dividend return (before dividend imputation) was 2.7% in the year to the end of 2008, and the best performance was 6.2% in the year to the end of December 2009, as recorded on the

ASX website. So, even in the scariest of economic conditions, for example a Global Financial Crisis, as a shareholder in industrial companies, you can expect at least some dividend return. Collected from a variety of different stocks, these add towards your gross passive income.

I estimate I'll typically get an average of 4% to 5% p.a. in passive income from my portfolio. Having an approximate idea of what the income will be – and being able to compare it to the previous year – gives me the motivation to keep building it and adding more shares to the portfolio. Eventually, it will compound enough to achieve my financial goal of covering my cost of living, providing me with the financial independence and freedom that I desire. This is so simple and something that you can do too!

## WHY SHARES?

One of the reasons I love investing in shares (and in particular Australian industrial shares, if you hadn't noticed yet), is that it's so quick and easy to get started. You can buy shares with as little as $500! However, there's typically a 'brokerage' or transaction fee of around $20 to buy each parcel of shares (using a DIY online broker such as CommSec or ANZ Share Investing), so I suggest starting with $1000 worth so that your investment doesn't get eaten away by these fees.

Compare this to property, where it could take you years and years just to save up a deposit – buying shares means that you can get started on your investment journey much sooner and start building momentum. Also, you don't need to worry about the exorbitant stamp duty that we have to pay on property in Australia, nor the eroding holding costs such as strata fees, landlord's insurance, water and council rates.

If you want to sell some of your shares down the track, you can do so relatively easily and quickly as well, and you don't have to sell the entire portfolio just to release a certain amount of money. By contrast, you can't sell a third of an investment property – it's all or nothing.

*I suggest starting with $1000 so that your investment doesn't get eaten away by these fees*

And when you do sell property, the exit costs are quite high, with legal fees, agents' commissions, marketing expenses and so on . . . Not to mention that it can take more than a few months to sell by the time you advertise the property, have the inspection campaign, and get through to the exchange of contracts and settlement period. With shares, you just pay a brokerage charge – either a flat dollar amount or a small percentage of your profits – and then the money turns up in your bank account within two business days.

But what I love probably most of all about Australian shares is that most industrial shares come with what are called 'franking credits'. Franking credits (also known as 'imputation credits') are a type of tax credit that allow Australian companies to pass on any tax that they have already paid (at the company tax rate) to the shareholder. The shareholder can then use this prepaid tax as a credit to help reduce their income tax (and potentially receive a tax refund, depending on their marginal tax rate).

Let's look at an example to show how this works.

Say you earn $400 in passive income from your portfolio of Australian industrial shares via dividends, and a further $400 from your term deposit via the interest you've earned. Both investments are earning you the same income: $400 each.

However, the dividend from your shares comes with a franking credit, as tax at the company rate of 30% has been paid to the ATO by the company on your behalf. The interest earned from your term deposit, however, comes with no tax credits.

When you do your taxes, you naturally (and honestly) declare both sources and amounts of passive income; for the dividend income, you add the tax credit back in to your total declared taxable income. I've put the figures into a table for you:

|  | Shares | Term Deposit |
|---|---|---|
| Income | $400 | $400 |
| *Plus* franking credit | $171 | $0 |
| Total taxable value | $571 | $400 |

In your hand, you've received the same income from the shares as from the term deposit – $400. However, after income tax is factored in, the numbers shift. If you had a marginal tax rate of 40%, for example, you'd owe $228 in tax on your dividends, versus $160 on your interest from your term deposit. But you get to use your magic franking credits on the dividend income, and deduct the tax that was previously paid by the company ($171) from the tax you owe ($228) – leaving you only owing the tax office $57. With the interest earned on the term deposit, by comparison, you have to pay the full $160 in tax, as there's no tax credit. Here's how it looks in our table:

|  | Shares | Term Deposit |
|---|---|---|
| Income | $400 | $400 |
| *Plus* franking credit | $171 | $0 |
| Total taxable value | $571 | $400 |
| Less tax @ (say) 40% | -$228 | -$160 |
| Add back franking credit | $171 | $0 |
| Net tax payable | -$57 | -$160 |
| Total income after tax | $343 | $240 |

So, at the end of the day, your net position from investing in shares with dividends that have franking credits is higher: you're walking away with $103 more.

As you can see, Australian industrial shares with franking credits can be extremely valuable in your portfolio, especially when you look at the after-tax returns – and the amount of money left over in your pocket.

Franking credits are the reason that industrial shares outperform resources and even the All Ords over the long run – these valuable tax credits are typically not available in the resources sector of the sharemarket.

For the $1000 Project portfolio, I've removed temptation where possible and enrolled in automatic dividend reinvestment plans for all the companies that have them. This way, I don't need to remind myself not to accidentally spend any of my precious passive income, and put it to better use for the future. For the companies that don't offer automatic dividend reinvestment plans, I make sure that I immediately transfer any dividends paid to my separate $1000 Project account, and then buy more stocks once I have another $1000 ready to invest.

At any point, you can decide to stop reinvesting the dividends and simply receive them as payments to your bank account. It's quick and simple to change this – you have complete freedom and control.

Looking at my growing passive income, I have zero intention of ever selling my $1000 Project share portfolio. It currently provides an annual income (albeit small), and if I can continuously

Having an investment plan where the funds automatically come out of your account without you having to remember helps to create a great habit.

reinvest the dividends for future compounding growth, and add to the portfolio by buying more stocks with my parcels of $1000 at a time, the passive income will grow over the long run and eventually cover my cost of living.

## OUTSOURCING SOME OF THE HEAVY LIFTING

The investment strategy that I'm talking about is a very simple 'buy and hold' one; the actual picking of the companies for your portfolio can be just as simple.

Now, investing opportunities don't just exist within the Australian sharemarket – the numbers are equally impressive for most international stock markets. So, to help me diversify and spread my risk (which I'll discuss further in the next section), I chose to get some expert assistance in the creation of my growing portfolio, including purchasing international shares.

I don't really feel like I have the expertise or knowledge necessary to pick individual companies to invest in outside of my own country – sometimes I'm not even 100% comfortable picking individual stocks within Australia. So, I often outsource this part of the decision-making process to an expert, by investing in an exchange traded fund (ETF) or even a listed investment company (LIC).

Both exchange traded funds and listed investment companies are prepackaged selections of shares, bundled into a single option that is traded together on the stock exchange. You buy ETFs and LICs like shares, and they pay dividends and have the same objective to grow in value over time as companies do. The key benefit is that you don't have to worry about choosing what stocks to buy and when: it's handled for you by whoever issues that particular ETF or LIC.

Each ETF and LIC has an inbuilt portfolio of shares that has been hand-picked by a fund manager, and is already diversified. In my case, an ETF or LIC was a great choice when I wanted to invest in the US market but had no idea of the best company to buy into, and only had a small amount of money to invest initially. An internationally based ETF or LIC allowed me to start building a portfolio with diversified exposure to the US stock market, without the stress.

There are plenty of Australian ETFs and LICs that also offer these benefits if you want to outsource your investment decisions. And in fact, I've incorporated a core strategy in the $1000 Project portfolio where I slowly add to my holdings of these styles of investments each time I have another $1000 to invest. Then I cherrypick individual shares to buy if and when I want. This makes investing very simple and a lot less stressful.

*the investment strategy I'm talking about is a very simple 'buy and hold' one*

Of course, in exchange for doing this heavy lifting and decision-making for you, ETF or LIC portfolio managers charge a predetermined fee. You have no say in which stocks you want and don't want in the portfolio, or when they are bought and sold. You also don't have any voting rights in the companies whose shares you own. Even so, ETFs and LICs are a terrific way to build a diversified portfolio if you want to get started but don't have the time to do all the research.

Another, similar option is managed funds. Just as with ETFs and LICs, a manager selects the stocks for the fund and decides if, when and how much they will purchase. Managed funds aren't traded on the stock exchange like ETFs and LICs, though, as your money is pooled together with those of other investors. Also, these types of funds aren't quite as popular or big as ETFs and LICs tend to be, and so the fees are higher – typically between 0.75% p.a. and 2% p.a. An ETF is more economical, with the fee range being more like 0.05% to 1% p.a.

So why would you use a managed fund over an ETF or LIC? Well, one advantage is that most managed funds allow regular investment through an automatic direct debit. You can invest an initial amount (typically the minimum is $5000) and then set up a regular investment plan of, say, $100 per month. This is great for people who want an almost 'set and forget' invest-ment strategy, where they don't need to deal with online broker accounts or stockbrokers, or pay brokerage fees every time they want to add to their portfolio.

Having an investment plan where the funds automatically come out of your account without you having to remember helps to create a great habit. Often, after enough time has passed, you don't even notice the money coming out, but you still get the comfort of knowing that you're building your financial future. And you can also set your account up to have your dividends automatically reinvested back into the managed fund, which gives you more opportunities for growth.

Not all ETFs and LICs allow automatic reinvestment, which means that you need to manually buy more yourself; you also have to make sure that you don't accidentally spend the dividends when they're deposited into your account. If your account is set up with the dividends going into your everyday spending account, they can soon evaporate into your weekly or monthly spending!

If you're an organised person and regularly check your bank transactions, transferring the dividends into your $1000 Project account is easy to do. For me, though, I find that life can get distracting, and an ETF or LIC with an automatic reinvestment plan is much easier to manage.

If you want to regularly add money to your ETF or LIC investment, you can set up a separate account where an automatic monthly amount is put aside until there's enough to invest. (As I mentioned earlier, I recommend waiting until you have $1000 or more, to keep the financial impact of brokerage fees down.)

The most important thing when it comes to picking a managed fund, ETF or LIC – or a stock! – is that you're clear on what your goals are, what your time frame for investing is, and how much of an appetite for risk you have. This will help you to work out where you should be investing your money to achieve your financial goals. Do your research and always read all the documentation before making a final decision.

## HOW MUCH RISK CAN YOU BEAR?

When I first started building my portfolio for the $1000 Project, I could only buy one parcel of $1000 worth of shares at a time. This meant that I carried a lot of investment risk in the early stages, as the value and performance of my portfolio was heavily reliant on just a few different companies.

As time went on, though, I was able to add different shares to the portfolio, and soon I had ten to fifteen different stocks, operating in different industries, and all paying me dividends. Today, I have over eighteen different stocks and my aim is to continue to diversify my portfolio up to between twenty and twenty-five different stocks, before I go on to focus on building the number of units I hold in each company.

Having this range of different companies in my portfolio has really reduced my investment risk – it's spread across a wider range of businesses and industries, which helps protect me when some go through challenging periods. Whether you're buying direct equities (shares), ETFs, LICs or managed funds, it's important to remember that companies don't perform in a uniform manner. Profits, performance, risks, threats and opportunities vary from one business to another. Having a healthy mix of different shares means that the volatility or share-price pullbacks of a company that's struggling will be offset by the strength of other companies in your portfolio.

It's human nature to want maximum return on your money with minimal risk, but some people can handle more risk than others. To help you understand where your limit is and how it should affect your investing habits, I recommend doing a risk profile questionnaire. This is a series of questions about your investing experience, how you'd react to certain conditions and why, how you feel about investing, and so on. There are plenty of these questionnaires available online – one of my favourites is on the Vanguard website vanguardinvestments.com.au.

After you complete an online risk questionnaire, your answers are analysed and you're given your risk profile. Your profile may vary slightly from questionnaire to questionnaire, but each one will give you a feel as to where your portfolio or asset construction should sit. Risk profiles range from very risk averse (often called 'cash' or 'conservative' investors) through to more comfortable with risk ('growth' or 'high growth' investors). There's no right or wrong profile – they're purely designed to show which type of investment asset class will work best for you and your goals. And your profile may change as your level of experience and knowledge evolves.

But no matter what your risk profile turns out to be, please go back and look at the two charts on pages 117 and 118 – you can see from the charts why I've chosen to focus on shares.

The good news is that once you know your profile, you can start researching and finding different pre-constructed managed funds or ETFs that would be appropriate for you. Then you're on your way to building your investment portfolio!

it's human nature to want maximum return on your money with minimal risk, but some people can handle more risk than others

## RISK AND ASSET CLASSES

Your risk profile will suggest what percentages of different 'asset classes' you could aim to have in your investment portfolio in order to match the level of risk you're comfortable with. This could be, for example, 30% Australian shares, 35% international shares, 10% cash, 12.5% Australian fixed-interest investments and 12.5% international fixed-interest investments.

Asset classes can be divided into two groups:

1. **Income-based assets**, which are quite conservative, consistent and carry low risk, but also have low returns over the short to medium term. Examples include cash (as in savings) and fixed-interest investments like term deposits, corporate and government bonds, and so on. The returns are usually very reliable, so great for the nervous investor, but won't be enormous. Worst of all, these assets are missing the element of capital growth, which makes a big difference over the long run as to whether the income grows or keeps up with you.

2. **Growth assets**, which include assets such as property and domestic and international shares. These investments experience high levels of short- to medium-term volatility, so they carry more risk – but in the long term, the returns are generally much higher, particularly when you are properly diversified and manage your investments correctly. And remember, we want the growth assets that we invest in to pay an income, so that we get the best of both worlds.

With investments in growth assets, when market volatility kicks in and you watch your portfolio ride a tsunami of downs upon downs, you need to be able to calmly and rationally ride those waves, and become a professional surfer! You have to focus on the long-term results; you may even be able to capitalise on a downturn by grabbing a few bargains in the sharemarket's 'stocktake clearance sale'.

Think about it: how would you react if your favourite shop suddenly started selling its stock at a massive discount? Would you panic and sell all the items you previously purchased from that store? Umm . . . no. You'd probably hightail it to the store and make the most of the opportunity!

Just bear in mind, though, that a tsunami-style stocktake sale like this can go on for as long as two years, sometimes even longer. Which can be a true test of your strength and determination, as well as your trust in yourself and your decision to invest in this asset class. You need to focus on your strategy and stick to it. And don't forget, if you have dividend-paying shares, even when those share prices are supressed, you will most likely still be earning a passive income from those shares. So they still have your back in the tough times.

More advanced investors tend to view income-based assets as boring and slow in comparison to growth assets, and much prefer the thrill, excitement and opportunity or even efficiency that growth assets provide. But income-based assets have a very valid place in the investing world. They're often a suitable choice for people who have a shorter investment time frame, for example, as the volatility risk is reduced.

Let's say you have $20 000 to invest and your goal is to buy a new car in five years' time. Even though your instincts and risk profile indicate you're better suited to being a growth or even high-growth investor, you don't have the benefit of time on your side – you want to be able to spend this money within five years. So, you'd be wiser to keep it invested in something simple and, most importantly, liquid (can be sold quickly), like cash. That way, when you're ready to purchase the car, the money will be there ready for you, and hopefully will have grown to more than you invested initially, even if only by a little.

If you put that $20 000 in an aggressive high-growth port-folio, and in year four the Australian stock market experiences a correction or pullback for whatever reason, the value of your investments could drop with the market. That $20 000 could be suddenly worth only $16 000 (a loss of $4000), and your time to buy the car is approaching, meaning you have to crystallise that loss by selling the portfolio. If you crystallise your loss, it means that you have formally locked in and confirmed that loss. You haven't given it the time or benefit of the doubt to recover. So, unless you have a long-term goal at least seven years away – or, even better, a minimum of ten – be careful about including too many growth assets in your portfolio.

Typically, the younger you are, the more time you have to invest, the more opportunities you may want to take to give your funds a chance to grow in value – and the more risk you may be able to bear. The general consensus is that younger people should focus more on long-term wealth opportunities, and should have a portfolio closer to the growth or even high-growth end of the spectrum.

It doesn't work like this for everyone, though. If you're completely new to investing, you may want to start with a more balanced approach, and then look to slowly add more growth assets to your portfolio as time goes by and more parcels of $1000 flow in. You can let it evolve and grow organically with your experience and education levels. Remember: the choice is yours, and this is your money, so you need to be comfortable with what you decide to do.

*Typically, the younger you are, the more time you have to invest . . . and the more risk you may be able to bear*

On that note, if you're doing the $1000 Project initially to fix short-term financial problems such as paying off debt, but you feel inspired and motivated by the simplicity and effectiveness of investing and are eager to get started, the good news is that you can! Start with your superannuation.

Your superannuation is actually your own investment portfolio, which is simply locked by the government so that you can't spend it. If you're an employee, your employer is paying 9.5% of your salary every year into this locked investment portfolio for you. And you can decide where it gets invested.

Most likely, your superannuation account will eventually become your primary source of retirement income, so it pays to invest in it and help it grow wisely. Refer back to charts one and two and ask yourself – where would you like your money invested for your future? The build-up for retirement for many Australians is at least thirty to forty years, so you may have the benefit of time, depending on your age and circumstances. And the more money that you have in super, the greater the income you will be able to draw in retirement, or the longer the income will last. Both sound good to me.

So, do yourself a huge favour and involve yourself with where your superannuation is invested today. Don't settle for the default account because you're too busy to check. Call your super provider and see where your money is invested and what other options exist. (Again, refer to charts one and two for inspiration if the sharemarket is within your comfort zone.)

In the meantime, use the $1000 Project to achieve your other financial goals and come back to investing later if you want to. Just don't neglect your super!

# HOW TO GET STARTED IN SHARES – 5 EASY STEPS

In summary, if you intend to use the $1000 Project to start investing, you need to follow these steps:

1.  Understand your goals.
2.  Complete a risk profile questionnaire, but remember to assess it while looking at the two charts in this chapter.
3.  Consider different investments, including managed funds, ETFs, LICS and even shares if you feel up for them. Remember, the first three options take away the stress and reduce the time you need to spend researching.
4.  Make a decision and implement it.
5.  Review your portfolio regularly, but focus on the passive income that it's generating rather than the growth, and look to improve and build this as much you can.

Most importantly – never stop growing your financial knowledge and experience!

# CHAPTER EIGHT

# Rest, Revive, Reward

I sometimes think I should have called the $1000 Project the $1000 *Challenge*. If you've set yourself a powerful enough goal, the project will sometimes be a real test of your mental and emotional resilience. However, while the emotions sometimes come out of nowhere, you can change them with the flick of a switch if you learn how to channel them to your advantage.

For me, the $1000 Project was hard work. I went to bed thinking about what I needed to do to come up with the next $1000, and woke up wondering how and when I was going to come up with a new parcel. It consumed me. I'd get frustrated if my current $1000 manifested slowly, and then I'd get an exhilarating high when some parcels of $1000 freely and easily flew in.

I loved the feelings of achievement and accomplishment each time I purchased some shares, ticking the parcel off my list and seeing the increase in my passive income. But there were also times when I was exhausted and bored – I was sick of thinking about it, talking about it and doing it!

This roller-coaster of emotions went on for the entire twelve months. I think I drove my family and friends nuts talking about it with so much determination, stress, confusion and, at times, anxiety. I felt like this project was my baby: my passion to help other people and to lead by example meant that I wasn't just financially invested, I was emotionally invested as well. I wanted to show people how to open their minds and to realise their potential, to show that money can be created and earned beyond our salaries, and that we all deserve financial freedom and harmony in our lives. And I wanted to do it honestly, openly and with complete transparency so that people could see it for themselves. I'd put a lot of pressure on myself!

And then, when I finally hit my first twelve-month deadline, I fell short of my ultimate goal. My aim had been to build a passive income of $2000 p.a. I got to $1750. It was such a small gap, but I felt disappointed.

It was hard to swallow – I'd come so close but hadn't quite got there. As I sat with that disappointment, though, a sense of relief began to emerge, and then a feeling of peace. I knew that I could take a little breather and reassess my goals and my methods for the project, and even sharpen my axe for round two.

And *then* I realised that I was actually really chuffed with myself and my accomplishments! I'd set myself a tough goal, with strict rules and guidelines, and I'd stuck to them. I felt pride knowing that I'd done everything I could to make the project as successful as possible. I was proud that I'd abided by my rules, stuck to my goals, regularly reviewed my progress and constantly looked for ideas, opportunities and ways to improve. I could put my hand on my heart at the end of the twelve-month period and say with authenticity and contentment that I'd given this project everything I had.

Nothing great is achieved with ease. The $1000 Project was not always a walk in the park – and if it had been, that would've meant I was setting my bar too low and not really striving to the level I could accomplish, or that I wasn't taking my goals seriously enough.

## dare to dream bigger, bolder and better

Falling short of my passive-income goal also made me a better goal-setter when it came to restarting the project for round two, as I knew what was realistically within my reach and how much to push my goal out so that I was continuing to grow. As discussed in chapter two, your goals need to be realistic, but also a challenge, so that you wake up the skills, mindset and attitude within you that will create what you want from the project.

If you find that you're coasting through, it means you need to up the ante! You either need to set yourself a closer deadline or make your goal bigger. You could aim to pay off your student debt sooner, save a bigger deposit, invest more regularly or build more passive income – the only person who misses out if you're complacent is you. If you find the project easy, go harder: you're selling yourself short and missing out on the golden nuggets of growth that come from hard work, passion, determination and challenges. So dare to dream bigger, bolder and better!

## PUSH THROUGH THE HARD TIMES

Back when I initially began the $1000 Project, I was excited, motivated and empowered. Ideas constantly came to me, some-times in a burst of several at once, and sometimes as just one great idea on its own. When I was in this stage, turning these ideas into action was easy. I didn't stop to think and allow myself to come up with excuses; I just powered through. It was a great zone to be in and the feeling of simply getting things done and seeing my progress was addictive.

At other times, though, I would hit a low, where I ran out of ideas, or opportunities simply weren't there, such as when I real-ised that I had no more items to sell or I had no more weekend jobs that I could work on. The worst came when people didn't honour payment for my weekend jobs or paid four months late . . . then feelings of frustration and stress kicked in, and my fear of failure rose. I juggled feelings of anger, disgust and disrespect, but learnt to shift that (with great effort) to feeling sorry for those people.

And, of course, there were times when I was simply bored or tired or just didn't feel like doing anything. When I really wanted to go to an expensive restaurant even though a local restaurant would have been more than enough, or to buy a new dress instead of wearing something that I already owned or borrowing a dress from a friend.

I went through slumps in motivation, too. Like whenever I put together a pile of items to be sold online for some extra cash. The pile could easily sit there for weeks, with me occasionally walking around it, coming up with excuses as to why I didn't need to put the items online right away, I could do it tomorrow – when another excuse would present itself!

But then I would review my deadline, see that valuable time was being wasted, and decide that I was not displaying the characteristics of someone who was serious about success. I'd tell myself to cut the crap, and that I was taking more time to come up with excuses than it would take to actually list the items. I would also focus on the freeing feeling I'd get once the items were gone (decluttering my home is a favourite pastime!), and the satisfaction of seeing the fresh earnings sitting in my account.

When I was feeling stressed, frustrated or demotivated, I would sit with the feeling, listen to what my body was trying to tell me, and use it as an opportunity to recharge my batteries, check in with myself, give myself the nurturing I needed, and then bring my focus back to my goal. Sometimes I knew I needed to take a break for a week, or to buy or do something nice for myself – but nothing too extravagant. I didn't want to undo all of my hard work and progress!

These 'treats' were simple, quick and easy things, such as getting a facial, or taking the night off cooking to enjoy home delivery. If I needed it that badly in order to get back on the path again quickly, it was allowed. After all, we aren't robots – we have emotional needs and wants.

Once I'd listened to my mind and body and given it what it needed to feel re-energised, I would remind myself why I'd set the goal in the first place. What was it that made me set the goal? How would I feel when I achieved this goal? What would it take to know that I gave it my absolute everything and to be able to look back with pride?

I'd also ask myself what key characteristics I'd need to have to be a successful person for the $1000 Project. Just listing in my head these positive qualities – energetic, inspiring, motivated, organised, in control, proactive, creative – would help to gently encourage me to get out of the dangerous zone.

These simple questions were enough to create the shift and help me to feel connected again to my goal. I never let the feeling of being 'off' continue for too long, as I knew that it was eating into my valuable time, which would then create more pressure and stress, breeding even more dissatisfaction and reasons for failure.

When I was feeling stressed, frustrated or demotivated, I would sit with the feeling, listen to what my body was trying to tell me, and use it as an opportunity to recharge my batteries.

And one thing that I never did was berate myself. I never bullied myself, or gave myself a hard time, or told myself I was being lazy. I always approached the project from a place of support and self-love – like I was my own inner life coach!

Negative self-talk when it comes to personal challenges serves no good. Quite the opposite, in fact – it can keep you stuck in a toxic, defeatist place where you completely stop growing. And no one is any good to anyone when they're operating in a place like that. You need to trust yourself and know that you have everything within you to complete this project and make it a success for you.

So if you catch yourself falling into that place, stop, take a break, and remind yourself of what made you decide to do the $1000 Project in the first place. Why is the goal that you set so important to you? What are you going to feel when you achieve it? Pride, achievement, relief, freedom? How are you going to celebrate when you reach your deadline? What's going to be your reward for successfully completing the $1000 Project?

Another good way to motivate yourself could be to start thinking about what you want your *next* goals to be. If you're using the $1000 Project as a way of getting out of debt, for example, it's easy to feel that all your hard work is going to something not very exciting. Focus on the next step: once you've achieved your highest priority goal, then you can get stuck into a fresh new goal that could be more meaningful for you, such as starting to save or even investing. This can help to trigger excitement and energy for you, as the money that you're creating will actually remain with you rather than going towards paying off something from your past.

Sometimes these difficult moments can be very valuable, as feelings that you might have buried deep finally come to the surface, bringing with them wisdom and awareness. If you're using the $1000 Project to get out of toxic debt, such as credit card debt, you'll find yourself confronting the reality of just how bad this type of debt is, and how destructive it is for your hopes of building wealth and financial security. It's healthy to discover this – letting the feelings come to the surface and being able to acknowledge them is how you'll learn to sit comfortably with them, and then to let them go. And hopefully this gives you the push to replace old, bad spending habits with new and positive ones that will serve you financially and holistically. You can use these waves of emotions to learn more about yourself and grow.

## DON'T BE AFRAID OF FAILURE

As I was doing the project, sometimes I would experience setbacks that were out of my control. Once, when I was in the middle of a drought and feeling a little frustrated, I was given an opportunity to do some market research for $240. I really appreciated this as it gave me the opportunity to finally get the current parcel that I was working on – ever so slowly – to the point of completion.

The market research session was on a Thursday evening, and the call came through at the last minute. This meant that I wouldn't be able to have dinner with my son, which is one of my favourite times of the day, as we take time out of the busy week to cook and eat together. Fortunately, my parents very kindly offered to have dinner with Rocco so that I could go.

That evening it was absolutely pouring. I already felt flustered as I picked Rocco up from day care, quickly got him home into the bath and his pyjamas, rushed him over to my parents, and then headed straight to the office where the market research was being held.

*you can use these waves of emotions to learn more about yourself and grow*

In spite of this, though, I felt prepared for the job. Part of my task was to do some homework, which I had diligently completed and packed in my handbag. And I'd looked up the location and estimated travel time, allowing for peak-hour traffic and time to find a parking spot, while still being five minutes early as requested.

But the traffic was horrendous. It was cold, dark and wet. The trip that was supposed to take me twenty-two minutes took over an hour. I rang the phone number given by the market research company to let them know that I was on my way, but there was no answer. I finally got there, parked and bolted inside, holding my homework close to my chest so that it didn't get wet. There was no one around except a sign that read: 'If you are here for market research, please take a seat in the waiting area and someone will come to collect you.'

I waited for twenty-five minutes in the empty office. No one came, and I ended up heading back into the rain to sit in more traffic and head back over to the other side of town to pick up my son and take him home to bed.

I was tired, hungry and so annoyed at myself. I'd missed out on finishing this irritatingly slow $1000; I'd spent the evening rushing around to try to make this happen; and, hardest of all, I'd missed a night with Rocco. I was too exhausted to even cry.

I'd tried my best but it was out of my hands, and I had to accept that and move on to the next opportunity. But that experience also made me realise where my boundaries lay, and what I was and wasn't prepared to give up in pursuit of the $1000 Project. While I made up the quality time to Rocco, I decided that, from that point on, missing out on quality time with my son was not worth it. It was a good boundary for me to discover, and since then I feel no guilt when I make decisions not to sacrifice time with Rocco.

Whatever negative feelings, disappointments or setbacks you experience while doing this challenge, just keep persevering. When these hard moments happen (and I guarantee they will), it doesn't mean that it's time to give up. They're simply bumps along the way, and stopping would be selling yourself short.

And, on the positive side, there will also be times when you have incredible strength and energy and feel intrinsically connected to your goal. When you're riding these powerful waves, keep riding them. Keep creating more success, and then stop when you need to. And when you're tired and exhausted, those are the nights that you head to bed early.

Incredible growth and strength comes from accepting what you're feeling, giving your mind and body a quick but replenishing pit stop, and then soldiering on. But you only realise you've received this gift of growth when you look back from the point of completion, and realise just how much strength and determination exists within you when you need it.

After I'd finished round one of the $1000 Project, I took a much-needed break to recharge and relax and have some time back for myself – and then I realised that I actually missed the project. I missed the test and the challenge, I missed the new-found awareness that I was building, I missed seeing how far I could go if I pushed myself. I missed the feeling of pride in seeing what I was building, and the excitement of being able to show people how to do this for themselves, how to discover their own strength and improved financial awareness and security.

And so, after only a few months' break, I found myself setting new goals and coming up with new ideas and hit lists for round two. I felt kind of lost without the $1000 Project in my life, and I craved the new world of discoveries, purpose, deeper self-awareness and exciting opportunities that I could create and capture for more financial stability, freedom and harmony.

*realise just how much strength and determination exists within you when you need it*

# CHAPTER NINE

## My Big, Bold Vision

When I find myself getting caught up in the materialistic, shallow stuff that can infiltrate our day-to-day lives, I try to remind myself of this: we come into this world with nothing and leave with nothing. Spending your life building up a financial fortune without sharing it or using it to make a difference would be, in my view, selling yourself short. We need to see the big and beautiful picture, and I think it's our duty to create something bold and powerful that we can leave behind.

We all have the ability to help others, whether in a big or small way. The same amount of power and strength to be a force for good exists within all of us – it's just a matter of actually *doing* something with it. Even if it's just a little something, it all helps and can make a difference.

And when we give to charity or help someone or something in need, often we get soul-filling and healing actions in return. This shouldn't be our sole intention, but often in giving, we do gain much-needed perspective. And that kick up the backside reminds us how lucky we are, and that we should be grateful for all we have.

Giving is empowering and strengthening, and can play a part in curing loneliness, as part of giving is connecting. Not just with a person or a charity, but with ourselves and our values.

I also think that when you give, you have to give unconditionally – don't have any expectations, just give happily and step back. That's the most admirable way of giving to me: privately. If you expect praise, fame or even appreciation when you give, you aren't giving wholeheartedly, and you're setting yourself up for disappointment. The blessing in charity is in giving with no strings attached.

*we all have the ability to help others, whether in a big or small way*

And helping someone or giving to charity doesn't need to necessarily be about giving money. It can also be about giving time or physical help, or helping to create awareness. In fact, giving your time is often more helpful and powerful than handing over cash, especially if you're able to help to raise money, build connections or develop access to better resources. It's all about working out where your power lies.

For the $1000 Project, I made the decision to donate the year's worth of passive income that my portfolio generated to a charity of my choice. I didn't want the $1000 Project to be purely about financial gains or 'getting rich'. I wanted to go deeper than this and look at wealth on a more genuine level, where our own financial fortune can be shared with others and help to spread care, connection, love and simple assistance. If we have the ability to change and improve our own lives, why not also do this for others in need?

When I realised that I was adamant about including a charitable purpose in the $1000 Project, it gave me so much joy and energy. After pausing to reflect on my life, I realised how lucky I am to be healthy and educated, and to have loving, caring people around me. Thinking about how grateful I was for everything I had, I decided it was time to put my hand in my pocket and give back. And it wasn't just about giving money away – I wanted to practise complete mindfulness in how I gave and to do it unconditionally.

I was working hard to earn that money, making so many sacrifices to build the portfolio and its passive income. I knew I'd

Thinking about how grateful I was for everything I had, I decided it was time to put my hand in my pocket and give back.

be taking a big step back by giving the money away, and that I'd possibly be jeopardising my ability to show others the magic of compounding interest, as I wouldn't have the passive income to keep reinvesting. So I knew that I had to make the decision consciously and wholeheartedly.

Thinking about it like this opened my mind to the possibilities and capabilities that existed within me to give back. And, if anything, it just made me more determined to succeed at the $1000 Project. Knowing that the more passive income I generated, the more I could give, my motivation to save harder and invest more grew stronger.

That decision point, to use this challenge to support a charity of my choice, was a huge *aha* moment. I realised that the $1000 Project was no longer just about saving and earning, but that I could also build a new and potentially extraordinary legacy with it. And I could help teach people not only to be more mindful about spending, but also to be more mindful about giving back and contributing to their communities, the environment and our world. And this is something that I'm committed to doing for as long as I can. As long as I can financially afford to, every year I will donate 100% of the passive income from the $1000 Project investment portfolio to a different charity of my choice.

I intend to keep the $1000 Project going every year, so that each year, a new and important charity is supported – with the donation getting bigger and bigger each time. This will improve its impact and benefits and allow me to help more causes and more people.

## FIND A CAUSE THAT HAS MEANING FOR YOU

Just like we can shop without truly being present, mindlessly putting stuff into our carts without pausing to think if we really need, will use or will even appreciate these items, sometimes we can take the same approach when giving to others. If we give to a charity, we should understand why we picked that particular one, what it means to us and why it's worth our support. We should also know where that money goes and what amazing work that charity does.

When I started to think about the first charity that I wanted to support, I realised that I had complete freedom to research and select a cause of my choice. This ignited a desire in me to really understand why I would pick a particular charity, and what made that charity so special and personal to me.

The first charity that came to mind was the Gidget Foundation. The Gidget Foundation was started in honour of a young mother who was secretly battling postnatal depression, which not even her closest family members knew about. Sadly, she took her own life. Her family and friends started the foundation to help create a safe haven where other mothers could go for help, support and strategies to help them cope with the passage into and through motherhood.

This is something that I hold close to my heart, as I too suffered from severe post-traumatic stress disorder, which was triggered by postnatal depression when I had Rocco. It was a very dark and frightening period of my life. I felt worthless, like a shell of who I am today, and deep down I just wanted to step away and not be a nuisance to anyone any more.

Fortunately, the right people picked up on the warning signs and got me help, and, most importantly, I learnt to help myself and I made a decision to heal myself. I am eternally grateful for those people in my life. Slowly, day by day, through the setbacks and triggers that are part of the natural healing process, I rebuilt my strength, my belief in myself and my attitude. And, in fact, creating and doing the $1000 Project really helped, as it gave me a positive distraction. Today, I'm loving life more than I ever have before and I have a sense of gratitude that I would never had experienced without going to that dark place earlier.

Looking back now, I can see that I gained awareness, growth, insight and mindfulness from this dark period of my life.

*if we give to a charity, we should understand why we picked that particular one, what it means to us and why it's worth our support*

It gave me depth of character and incredible strength. Without a doubt I still have tough days, and negative thoughts can creep into my head when things go wrong, people hurt me or triggering moments occur, and sometimes I even fear that it may come back. But I have the awareness now to catch these dark thoughts, and catch them quickly. And then I know to do the things that I need to let those emotions pass by, whether that be having a nap, meditating, using positive self-talk, eating a healthy meal, going to the gym, or – one of my fastest 'snap out of the head-space' activities – listening to a motivational talk on YouTube.

Reflecting on this period of my life made me realise how important charities like the Gidget Foundation are for women who are struggling with postnatal depression. As I made my first donation to them, I felt proud. I knew that I had a real purpose and mission for the $1000 Project.

## SEE GIVING AS PART OF THE BIGGER PICTURE OF YOUR LIFE

As I continued through round two of the project, I started to wonder what my next charity would be. This time, instead of thinking too much about it, I decided that I'd let the universe show me when the time was right.

As part of my first $1000 Project, I set myself a 'Frugal February' challenge, during which I forced myself for one month to live a simple, essentials-only existence, with any money I saved out of my personal budget going towards my next $1000 parcel. This quickly taught me how mindless I was with my cash and spending, and it brought a sense of grounding and respect back into my life.

I expected the same great lessons when doing Frugal February in round two, but this time it was very different. I became angry, frustrated and annoyed, and felt so constricted. I was fed up with denying myself anything fun!

Towards the end of Frugal February, I was invited to go to a ladies' lunch. Being at the end of my tether from feeling like the world's biggest tight-arse and constantly saying no and sulking, I decided to go, even though it was totally against my rules. I listened to my body, as I promised I'd do, and knew that a catch-up with my friends might help settle my frustration and give me the respite that would recharge my focus to finish off Frugal February on a stronger note. So off I went to the lunch, albeit feeling a little guilty.

It was a ridiculously hot Friday afternoon in Sydney, and we were sitting in a beautiful restaurant by the water, sipping rosé. I was enjoying myself, but I still felt a tad guilty. Then a woman who knew one of my friends walked passed our table. We invited her to come and join us for a drink, and the moment she sat down, I realised that I was supposed to meet this person and hear her story. It was meant to be, and I realised how powerful the universe is when we open up. Let's just say the guilt evaporated!

The lady who sat down next to me was called Adayanti, and as she shared her story, our mouths were hanging open in awe.

Anything that we were previously complaining about seemed so insignificant.

Adayanti's grandparents were two orphans who met in an orphanage in Jakarta, Indonesia. After Adayanti's father and maternal grandfather passed away within a close period of time, her mother decided to return to the orphanage in memory of her parents and take over the running of it.

This orphanage is supported solely by donations from the public. And listening to the stories Adayanti shared about her mother's strength, determination and passion as well as the children she cared for, I immediately wanted to help her continue her incredible work, making a difference in so many precious children's lives.

In the past, when I wanted to donate to charity, I felt somewhat restricted and limited, and at times like I wasn't doing enough or understanding how my money was going to help exactly. But deciding that I would give the next year's dividend income from the $1000 Project to the Pa van der Steur Orphanage felt really good, and I was excited. I was able to hear about Adayanti's mother's goals for the orphanage, how she wanted to help the children who were brought to her. All of the children had been through things most of us hopefully will never have to experience. Any financial help that I could give would really make a difference for their futures. It felt real to help, and now I felt even more motivated to push harder so that the donation I could hand over would be as big as possible.

After meeting this young woman, I felt at peace about going to that somewhat indulgent lunch, knowing that something really powerful and positive had come from it. I made sure that I held on to the enthusiasm and determination to make that year's total dividend amount as big as I could.

*I felt even more motivated to push harder so that the donation that I handed over would be as big as possible*

After this turning point, I had more awareness and I felt calmer as I progressed through the project. Of course, things went wrong occasionally, as they do in all of our lives. But when they did, it simply didn't bother me like it would have previously. I started to look for an underlying lesson in whatever happened, so that I could grow from it. Then I picked myself back up and moved on to focus on the next positive thing.

## INVOLVE OTHERS IN YOUR ACTS OF CHARITY

During this period, I became more aware of my desire to give and how it was motivating me. I was still so excited about giving the year's total dividend income to the Pa van der Steur Orphanage, but my deadline wasn't until October, and that felt so far away. I wanted to do something sooner, but not necessarily giving money. I wanted to give in a more personal way, where I could feel more involved and more helpful.

Rocco and I had a trip booked to Bali for some much-needed quality time. There had been a lot of sacrifices in building up the portfolio and, on occasion, 'Rocco time' had been shortened. As painful as the guilt was, I know that when Rocco is old enough, he will understand why and be proud, particularly when he knows about the great causes the money is supporting, and maybe one day take over if he wants to.

Watching my child grow up in Sydney, I can't help but feel incredibly lucky. We're surrounded by beautiful beaches and parks, and we have access to amazing food and high-quality schools. But at the same time, kids seem to constantly want and ask for things. I listen to my child assume that when his toy breaks, we can simply buy another one; when he selects his muffin from our local cafe, we can get another if he doesn't like the flavour or, heaven forbid, drops it on the floor; and that Christmas time and birthdays are just about getting lots of toys. And lots of kids live in a cashless world, where money comes out of a magical wall (AKA an ATM).

I'm doing my best to explain, patiently, to Rocco that we need to take care of our belongings and that money needs to be respected. I believe it's our responsibility as parents to teach our children that it's okay and safe to experience the word 'no' being said, and to process the feeling of not getting something that we want. And I also want to teach him to give – and to show him *why* we need to give. In particular, I wanted Rocco to identify with other children who have different challenges that he may never face, and see how his own powerful actions of giving can bring a smile and helping hand to another little person's life.

So, in anticipation of our trip to Bali, we researched various charities there and ended up contacting the Jodie O'Shea Orphanage in Denpasar and asking if they would like any new toys – and, if so, what types of toys. They immediately replied and gave us a humble list.

I explained to Rocco (who was about to turn four) what an orphanage was and how it would be nice to give these special children some new toys. He didn't quite understand what I was talking about, so we headed to our nearest big toy shop and I let Rocco pick out $1000 worth of toys and put them in the shopping trolley.

Only once did he show interest in a toy for himself; for the most part he stuck to the list and selected toys for both boys and girls and a wide range of ages. He understood that these toys being purchased were not for him but to be given to a special little girl or boy, similar in age to him. I was so proud and impressed. And I realised that I'd underestimated our ability to inspire and educate our own children about the importance of giving unconditionally.

Also, by including Rocco in the process and having toys as the donation – something that he knew how to value – I felt that he understood the meaning and act behind this so much more than if we'd been donating cash.

When we arrived in Bali, we went to the orphanage with five full boxes of toys. The kids rushed over to rip open the boxes and Rocco helped hand them out. He was a little overwhelmed but he could see immediately how much this meant to them.

## GIVE CONSCIOUSLY AND MINDFULLY

I learnt an important lesson there as well, which is that if you want to help, don't assume what people need or want. Ask them specifically what they need most, and be open to the answer. Giving toys to the Jodie O'Shea Orphanage was a special moment that I will treasure forever, and they were something that was really needed. But in talking to the managers of the orphanage when we were there, I learnt that food was one of the biggest challenges for them. With 98 children in the orphanage, nearly 300 meals were served up every day, and that didn't include the teachers' and carers' meals. So part of that $1000 could have gone towards fresh food. The toys brought them a lot of joy and happiness, but I was reminded again of the importance of being mindful and conscious when giving to others.

As your financial strength, control and progress develops through the $1000 Project, I suggest that you look to include an act of giving back or helping in some form, whether it be financial or simply giving of your time. Make sure that it's special and has meaning for you, ask what is the best way you can help, and then help in the best way that you can with no expectations of getting anything in return. That is real charity.

One thing's for sure: when you give consciously and unconditionally, your motivation and desire to repeat the process is incredible. For me, not only was it a huge source of inspiration and motivation to keep focused and not stop, but it also made me even more conscious of what I buy, use and consume, so that next time I could be even more helpful with the $1000 Project annual donation.

Help in the best way that you can with no expectations of getting anything in return. That is real charity.

# CHAPTER TEN

# The Energy of Inspiration

As I have shared with you, there were moments where I felt run-down during the $1000 Project. Sometimes I wanted to give up, questioning why I was putting all this energy into it. Sometimes I even thought I was a fool for thinking I could do this in the first place! Was anyone even interested? Would this even help people? And worst of all, would I be laughed at as an embarrassment?

Whenever I came close to quitting, though, a sign would land in my lap. I'd receive an email from a subscriber, or someone would come up to me in the street, or would write on my Facebook page. They shared what the $1000 Project meant to them and how they were successfully using it to change their financial future for the better. This is what helped me to keep going.

Their stories touched me, amazed me, made me feel proud of them – and, most importantly, they inspired me. I'm honoured that some of these incredible people have agreed to share their stories with you in this book, so you can see for yourself how the $1000 Project can change your life.

---

*'I began healing myself emotionally and financially'*

Here's my story on how I started my $1000 Project. But before I start, here is some background. I have always worked, since I was 13 years old; I married young, had two wonderful sons; I got divorced and received absolutely no financial support from their dad.

I continued to work and even managed to complete college and get my BA in Business Management. After being single for five years, I remarried to someone I thought was my dream man. I continued to work until my youngest son's senior year in college. I felt like I needed to be there for my son that last year – I had been working so much, not getting home until seven. So I quit my job, feeling secure that my husband had my back. It was such a nice break not to have to work. I was not planning to stay unemployed: it was just temporary.

It so happened that five months later, a friend started his business and asked me to work for him. Being that I was going to work from home, I was excited. I was taking a major pay cut, and had no benefits, but I was okay with that because I knew that as the business grew so would my salary – and the major bonus was, I was making a little money and staying at home to watch my son.

About a year after that, my husband decided that he wanted a divorce. This really flipped my life upside down. I had quit my job at a major oil company, given up my pension, benefits, salary. We had built our 'retirement' home, which was way more than I could afford on my new salary. I felt discarded. My financial situation was in the dumps; all my future life dreams were just pulled from under my feet.

I found your channel because of a video . . . about how to heal a broken heart, or something to that effect. After my first divorce, I knew that I should not depend on any-one for my financial security – that's why I always worked and got my education – but when my second husband was so supportive and I felt secure, after nine years, I let my guard down. Slowly, I began healing myself emotionally and financially.

*Dolores*

*'It's not about being perfect: it's about being better'*

I stumbled across the $1000 Project and immediately I knew that this was something I could do and wanted to do! Reading Canna's first blog entries with her supreme focus on squirrelling away cash reminded me of how in my twenties I scrounged together the deposit for my first apartment, so I knew I could absolutely do this if I put my mind to it!

I was pumped and all I needed was a goal. I was excited about share investing and this had the advantage of being something I could involve my sixteen-year-old stepdaughter in, as she is just starting to show an interest in finance. However, after having a honest look at my finances and my family's goals, my most pressing need is to protect the deposit I have saved up for a family house. I had just received a bill for a $15 000 repair on our current apartment and I paid for this out of the house deposit, so my goal was to pay myself back this $15 000 within twelve months, so that I still had the full deposit for the family house and an intact emergency fund.

My challenge is that I'm currently on maternity leave with a newborn baby, and am living the very frugal lifestyle that comes with a tiny baby, a toddler and a teenager. Lunches, dinners out and drinks with friends are just not something I can do often right now, so there is very little to cut out!

How on earth was I to save, create, earn over $1000 a month when I spent so little and was already pretty responsible with my money?

I had devoured Canna's blog and I knew I too had a bunch of clothes to sell on eBay – and that made me a few hundred dollars pretty easily. I then did a massive declutter and sold a bunch of furniture. It felt great to be rid of this stuff that was not adding value to my life, as well making money. So far this has made me over $1000, and I think I can make another $1000, then I'll be out of stuff to sell! Such a great feeling to be achieving my goal, and my stepdaughter was surprised at how quickly the little things added up.

My next step was to be my own financial advisor, take the magnifying glass over my finances, and see how I could better manage my savings, my emergency fund and my house deposit. This is where I struck gold! By consolidating my bank accounts and making sure every single cent was in the account that would give me the best interest rate or saving rate, I saved well over $3000! I am never again going to take my eye off this activity!

Now for the tedious stuff . . . I went about ensuring that I got the very best deal on all of my recurring bills. I renegotiated my health, car and contents insurances, my phone plan, my cable TV ($588 there alone), and also my gas and electricity. I found a few dodgy late fees from the bank and this project gave me the motivation to call and have them reversed. This again added up to over $3000! Yay!

I could make these phone calls while my baby was sleeping and it felt great to still be contributing towards a lovely house for my kids to grow up in while spending time at home looking after them.

By now all the easy pickings had gone, but I'd made so much progress I was motivated to keep going and find more savings. I pulled out the budget and looked at our biggest expenses. With a family of five, our grocery bill is pretty big, so I thought I'd try shopping at Aldi. This did take some convincing to get my husband to go there, but on our first shop we saved $80 (it was a huge shop, as we thought we'd try everything, and can I say: nappies!) and we are now both converts. So far this has saved us $1000, and this one is just going to keep saving us money year after year. Also, I see one or two ladies in there like myself with our designer handbags and expensive clothes and I think, *Yep, she knows where to spend and where to save!*

I've tried a bunch of other stuff that has saved a little bit here and there. I've done spa days at home, I've done user testing online, I've bought some beautiful baby things second-hand on eBay for amazing prices, and washed the car at home for free – and discovered my little one loves this on a hot day. Entertainment that actually saves me money, winning!

Some of these tricks I will do forever, as they are simply no trouble and get a great result. Other expenses I find are indulgences I really appreciate, so I do them guilt free.

For instance, I love my designer handbags and the occasional designer shoe, so they are staying put, and bit of professional pampering is more enjoyable than my home spa treatments. However, I will now always spend a few minutes to get a better deal next time a bill renewal comes up, and I will always do a quick look for a second-hand product before purchasing new.

I've found this whole experience to be very motivating and it has reignited my interest in personal finance. I'm almost five months in and I've saved $9949 out of my target of $15 000. There really haven't been many downs, but sometimes I think, *How on earth can I find my next $1000?* When this happens, I look at my graph where I track how much I've already recouped. I think about how this supports my values of providing for my family and only having useful, beautiful things in my life and retiring a little bit early on a great nest egg. I also think about how my mum set a great example of living within your means for us kids. I hope I can set that example for my kids, especially my girls, and add to that an example of how to invest, not just save.

For me, it's not about being perfect: it's about being better. It's not about deprivation, it's about finding out what I value and spending time and money guilt free on that.

*Rachel*

*'I feel like anything is possible'*

When I first heard about the $1000 Project, I thought, *Wow, I can never do that . . .* Then I thought, *Maybe I can do a* $100 *Project . . .* I am on my own – my son is grown up and has left home, I earn a moderate/average income and own my own home with a mortgage – nothing left over.

I opened a new account and labelled it 'Passive Income'. Then, within a couple of days I received a refund of $350 for something and *WOW,* so I put it in the passive income account, very excited . . . Within a month I had over $1000 and since then I have made $4000 and have redecorated my house – new couch, new bedroom suite, new dining chairs and lots of throws and pillows and accessories. It's just beautiful and I am so excited; would never have had it otherwise . . .

This has meant so much to me, as I never ever thought I could do it – but my supposed $100 Project did become the $1000 Successful Project! I continue to keep doing the $1000 Project today and have my passive income account still going . . . The benefits for me are that I feel wealthy, I feel like anything is possible and can have the luxuries I want. I'm currently saving for a holiday.

*Tina*

*'Thank you for making us believe we can do this'*

My name is Lisa; I'm from Adelaide, I'm twenty-eight, married and have a gorgeous daughter, Ava, who turns two next month.

My story begins with my struggle with infertility; after three years of struggling to conceive with help, I fell pregnant.

My husband and I would love to have another baby, but unfortunately the treatment I need and had with my daughter isn't covered by Medicare and my private health only covers a certain amount – with a waiting period of twelve months.

We decided to start our own $1000 Project after watching other videos of yours, with our main goal being $7000 (more if we can!). But we found breaking it down into $1000 goals was much more manageable and keeps us on track and staying positive. We started at the beginning of March and already have $2500 saved. We've implemented so many money-saving ideas from a few different videos you've done and we have the biggest motivation: to have another baby and give our daughter a sibling.

I want to personally thank you for motivating us and making us believe we can do this.

*Lisa*

*'I can't wait to do it again!'*

I opened up a CommSec account last year. My intention was to learn about share trading and maximise a long-service-leave payout I'd received; however, I found the whole thing so daunting that I never made a trade. I just didn't know what to do, and was scared I'd make such a poor decision that I'd lose money.

Fast forward to March this year; I was eight months' pregnant with my first baby and I had just begun maternity leave. I came across SugarMamma.TV and was totally engaged with your approach to financial advice for trading . . . By breaking it down into $1000 parcels from passive savings!

I was keen to feel like I was contributing to my family's financial independence, despite not working for another twelve months. My partner and I would be relying on his wage once the government paid parental leave ended. Just like other women who have a baby for the first time, I'm sure I'm not alone in feeling odd about relying on my partner's income for the first time – and what this would do, not only to our bank account balance but also to the balance of the relationship. The $1000 Project seemed like a fun and achievable way for me to contribute to our financial independence without dipping into our lowered income.

So, first of all I looked at our budget and realised we had $700 saved for car registration – however, we'd sold that car in February! What a great start! Below is the full breakdown of our first $1000 parcel:

- $700 car registration no longer needing to be paid
- $30 private health insurance rebate
- $50 bond refund for bicycle locker I no longer used
- $90 loose coins taken to bank
- $30 saved from not buying freshly cut flowers for a get-together
- $100 refund for a purchase I decided I didn't need or want

And there you have it – our first $1000, which came together within a fortnight! It felt so good! Here was $1000 from cash that just seemed to manifest from thin air. And quickly at that. I started looking around the house to see what I could do to make my next $1000 . . . an outdoor setting which doesn't suit our house; shoes and clothes to sell on eBay; my (very) overdue tax return.

I used advice from one of your other videos to make my decision to invest this first parcel, which I did with confidence. I can't wait to do it again! I now have a six-week-old daughter and feel like I can put some attention back towards the $1000 Project. I can't wait to see how it goes . . .

*Stephanie*

*'I knew things needed to change'*

My name is Nicole and I've been following you on YouTube since September last year. I came across your story about the $1000 Project while scrolling through news.com.au one day. Immediately I was inspired by your love of the finer things in life, while also working towards financial freedom and being in control of your money. I think your story really resonated with me because I felt like my husband and I weren't in control of our finances.

In September last year I was really feeling like things had spiralled out of control. We had $58 000 (maybe a little more) in personal loan debt. Every single dollar was unsecured debt. I had given birth to twins three months earlier. The IVF treatment cost us around $25 000 out of pocket including travel, accommodation and food (we live in remote Queensland so each cycle was a 3600-kilometre round trip). While we were undergoing treatment, my husband injured himself on his motorcross bike and broke his ankle. He took three months off work unpaid and had no income protection insurance. This meant we quickly acquired $13 000 credit card debt.

I knew things needed to change – your story was a gift from the universe and I was quickly addicted to your YouTube videos. You were up with me most nights, every hour keeping me company while I fed the babies. Your message was so clear and so achievable. With the support of my husband I took on the $1000 Project and couldn't believe how quickly I was acquiring my parcels of $1000. Before I knew it we had $17 000 just sitting there (until I watched another video and quickly realised I needed to pay it off an interest-earning debt).

Here's how I did it:

1. **Budget** – I am thirty-one years old and this was the first time I had a budget: a clear idea of my actual cost of living. It was very confronting, yet motivated me even further. I pay our electricity, internet, phones and private health insurance each fortnight to avoid additional bills – our bills now arrive in credit.

2. **eBay** – I signed up and sold anything I didn't love, appreciate and value. I sold bundles of excellent quality baby clothes, Mimco wallets and bags I no longer used, Mimco nappy bag, breast pump and juice plus vitamins. Before I knew it, my PayPal account was over $1000!

3. **Emptied my closet** – I emptied my closet onto my bed and invited the girls from work over. I sold them all of my clothes I no longer loved, wore, needed, fit and made around $500.

4. **Meal planning** – this has been my biggest saving. Our family was spending $450 to $500 per week on groceries, eating out and coffees. I now plan every

meal and we no longer go out for dinner unless it's to celebrate a special occasion. Our spend per week has reduced to $250. It's so much more fun to make pizzas together and have a picnic in the front yard or to have friends over and make memories.

5. **Selling our second car** – we did own two cars: one family car to accommodate our children and a smaller car I'd owned for around seven years. It was in great condition, as I had owned it since new. My husband catches a company bus out to the mine site each day and I am a teacher at a school one kilometre from my home. We didn't need two cars. I hadn't driven the smaller car in seven months before I decided to sell it. This was $8000 in cash, and I saved $600 by selling it prior to paying registration the following month and $400 on insurance.

6. **I quit shopping** – I applied a minimalistic approach after cleaning out so much. Some days my husband would arrive home to six garbage bags of 'stuff' to take to the charity bin or the tip! I quit shopping for fun and only bought things I needed to replace.

7. **Short-term pain for long-term gain** – this has been another change that made a significant difference to our finances. My husband has always worked Monday to Friday 7 a.m. to 5 p.m. In mining, this is almost unheard of. It worked well with our family schedule and allowed for a lot of

weekend family time. My husband chose to change his roster and work a 14/7 shift – seven days 6 a.m. to 6 p.m., then seven nights 6 p.m. to 6 a.m., and then seven days off. This change came with an additional pay rise. The pain of the roster is worth the pleasure of achieving our goal of financial freedom and abundance.

8. **Cancelled the credit card** – I combined credit card debt with an unsecured debt and consolidated into a fixed-term, fixed-interest-rate, no-redraw $40 000 personal loan. This has stopped overspending and has reduced the stress of multiple payments.

9. **Minimalism** – I found that minimalism is so good for the mind, the soul and the bank account!

Between October and February, we saved $17 000 (and still went on our annual trip overseas). We decided to use that $17 000 to pay out an existing personal loan debt. Our personal loan debt balance has reduced from $58 000 to $33 000. I still cannot believe that between the $1000 project, taking a minimalistic approach and watching your amazing videos, we have been able to achieve this in such a short period of time. I feel like we now have a plan, we are in control and we are so much more appreciative of the money we have.

We now value our money, pay for everything in cash and save for little luxuries we want in envelopes stashed in our bedroom. Your advice has been amazing for not only our finances, but also our health and happiness. I cannot thank you enough for the gift you have given our family, and I'm so grateful you take the time to create videos sharing your knowledge of finance.

*Nicole*

---

*'Wish we had learnt something as practical as this in school'*

Hi Canna, just wanted to share our little story and the huge influence you have had on us.

We are three sisters based in Scotland who have been running a successful little teashop for the last five years. We have always been a cash-positive business and have always paid our fifteen members of staff on time; however, at times we have felt frustrated with our finances and sometimes we struggled to pay ourselves regularly, fearing the next month wouldn't be so good! As young females, we found getting credit or business loans awkward, as we were not confident talking about money or asking for good discounts, so renovations or big purchases were always saved for and paid fully in cash upfront. Although it means we have no debt, we were not smart in the lean startup years.

We found your YouTube channel and your videos became our lectures, your recommended books became our reading lists, and we began to focus on what we wanted from the business and get creative with finding other ways to make more money. Watching your videos allowed us to realise how much we have accomplished, and your lifestyle tips have allowed us to integrate our work into our lives in a less consuming but more rewarding way.

We started the $1000 Project in order to make sure we could pay for some improvements in the cafe and sometimes a little treat for ourselves (a spa afternoon or a really nice meal, or a designer treat).

It was in doing this project that we unknowingly stumbled on our newest business, Sconebox. We are known locally for our freshly baked scones, which we make every morning. To make extra money, we came up with a way to package the dried ingredients and sell them to customers to make at home. The extra income grew and so did the idea – to create a baking subscription that not only included the scone blend but also tea, jam, napkins, a baking utensil and an artisan sweet or chocolate – everything to have a tea party! Sconebox hasn't officially launched yet but we already have great orders and more subscribers than we can believe, and such confidence dealing with 'men in suits' talking about finances.

We only wish we had learnt something as practical as this in school. Love what you're doing and love that you're doing it in such a unstuffy manner.

*Geraldine, Michelle & Jennifer*

*'The $1000 Project has healed my negative
relationship with money'*

Growing up in a household that lived week to week and never saved a cent, I fell into this pattern as an adult.

I felt so insecure about money. By the time I had my second child, I needed this to change. My financial stress was affecting my marriage and personal happiness.

I had started making better financial decisions, but I still had a long way to go towards feeling financially secure when I discovered Canna's YouTube channel. (I was one of the first 1000 subscribers!) I felt so inspired by Canna and her attitude towards money. I watched her videos religiously and took notes.

My main challenge with the $1000 Project was getting started. I had very limiting beliefs such as 'I don't know anything about stocks' and 'I am not someone who is good with money', which took time to resolve.

My goal is to have my own nest egg to fall back on in retirement. No one knows what the future holds, but I know that having my own long-term, diverse portfolio will give me some peace of mind.

I am raising my first $1000 by selling unwanted items on eBay and using all my affiliate income from my beauty blog. Even though the money is only coming in little bits, it's so exciting to see my $1000 Project account growing.

The $1000 Project has healed my negative relation-ship with money, given me a feeling of security and best of all: hope.

I can't thank Canna enough for all the information and inspiration she has given me and I can't wait to read the $1000 Project book!

*Lisa*

---

*'I had finally found a happy medium between*
*spending and saving'*

I always considered myself a good saver. While living at home and studying at university, I was eager to work as many shifts as I could manage at my various part-time jobs, so that I could put the money towards my next over-seas trip.

As soon as I entered the world of full-time work and started earning a salary, my attitude towards money changed. Very quickly, my desire for 'things' and keeping up with the latest trends consumed me, and I found myself browsing high-street stores multiple times per week (both in store and online), and purchasing an extensive amount of unnecessary items for myself. During this time, I also moved out of home and into a rental property, meaning that my cost of living increased substantially.

Looking back, I realise that this is the point in time when I should have reined in my shopping addiction to compensate for the additional expenses I now had in my life. Instead, I continued to shop and entered more dangerous waters . . . I started shopping for home decor! My willingness to save as much money as I could per fortnight had drastically diminished, and making a trip to the shops excited me beyond belief. However, at the same time I began to feel overwhelmed at the amount of choices I had and started to experience immense guilt every time I purchased something 'extra' for myself.

Reality hit me when some of my friends began to buy their first homes and I didn't have nearly enough money for a deposit of my own.

It wasn't long after having this realisation that I stumbled across SugarMamma.TV on YouTube. After viewing video upon video, I was extremely inspired by the wise words of Canna Campbell and motivated to change my attitude back to that of saving as much money as I possibly could. I promptly completed a budget and discovered that I could be saving an extra $200 per fortnight. I then established two financial goals – the first being to save $10 000 by the end of 2017 to put towards a deposit for my first home, and secondly to make one voluntary payment per month to reduce my HECS debt, or student loan.

My motivation to commence the $1000 Project was higher than ever. I immediately pulled everything out of my wardrobe and drawers. I filled multiple garbage bags with unloved clothing, footwear and bags that would either be donated to charity or sold. I then went to every room in the house and completed the same process in order to minimise my belongings and find extra savings. I investigated how to use Gumtree and eBay and furiously began taking photos and uploading items online. I sought out a local carboot sale and signed up for the next month's sale. I also registered with an organisation to participate in market research in an effort to earn extra cash.

I made changes to my spending habits by making a conscious effort not to purchase the 'little things', as they were seriously adding up and making a dent in my bank account. I stopped re-purchasing beauty products before I had used up all of the contents; I took lunch to work every day; and started driving to social events more often to save money on transportation and alcohol. I changed my standard credit card to an awards card in order to reap more benefits, and I researched in depth how I could use loyalty cards to my advantage. I embraced 'Frugal February' with all my strength, and spent my money sparingly for the next few months.

I continued in this money manifestation zone for four months and successfully saved an additional $2000! I finally realised what I was capable of achieving and slowly began to loosen my grip so that I could still treat myself occasionally and not completely exclude myself from my social circle.

I had finally found a happy medium between spending and saving.

I am proud to say that I have just made my first voluntary payment towards my HECS debt and I am empowered to continue saving as much as possible so that the deposit for my first home grows consistently over the next few years. The knowledge I have gained through SugarMamma. TV has been invaluable and as a result, I know that I will experience lifelong financial benefits.

*Rhian*

---

*'Thank you for helping make finance seem not so scary!'*

I have been following you on YouTube since you started! I absolutely love your channel and want to thank you for helping make finance seem not so scary!

I began doing your $1000 Project last January. I was fed up with my disorganised and cluttered closet and always spending my money on unnecessary things. (I definitely have a shopping addiction! I love fashion.) I finally had enough and started my journey by going through every item of clothing that I owned and donating/selling on Poshmark whatever I didn't need anymore. This process not only gave me so much space in my closet, but also put some money in my pocket. I put this money right into an account that I nicknamed 'My $1000 Project'.

After that first step, I was on a roll! I would make coffee at home instead of going to Starbucks and I would transfer that money right into my $1000 Project account. The money kept adding up!

I must say, this whole process was addictive. I keep trying to find more and more ways to cultivate money as well as save in other areas, just so I can see my savings grow. As of today, I have saved $2700 by doing the $1000 Project! And I am still going. This money is going into an account to save for a down payment on my first home. The $1000 Project has inspired me to live life in a more budget-friendly way, without being 'cheap' all of the time. I want to thank you, Canna, for the inspiration on this journey.

*Amanda*

---

*'A woman with confidence is strong, but a woman with confidence and wealth is unstoppable'*

Okay, so we are a family of three – my husband and I separated in August 2016, and in 2017, it is the year of 'attacking debt'. I have two amazing daughters – Joanne, aged six, and Emily, aged three, and we are currently in our second $1000 challenge.

**Our goal** – to be debt free by the end of 2017, so that we can save for a deposit on a house.

**How we are doing this** – our matrimonial home is on the market and we know that our next home will be smaller. So Gumtree is our new best friend – we have sold furniture, baby items and books, which has generated $630 this month. We have a princess tin moneybox which Joanne and Emily deposit the money straight into, and we cannot open it until 1st June 2017. Also, while the girls are with their father, I'm an Uber driver – so any profit (revenue minus expenses) I receive from Uber I withdraw . . . and Joanne and Emily deposit it once again into our moneybox.

**Rules for the $1000 challenge** – this money cannot be taken out of my full-time wage; it has to come out of the sales or income generated in other areas.

**Why include the girls** – to set good money habits in life early, I withdraw the money so Joanne and Emily know what $1000 looks like in the moneybox. We have named our debt monster 'Bill', and we are slowly killing Bill in every way possible. Joanne and Emily come with me to physically pay off these bills (no electronic transfer from our bank). This helps them understand the concepts of money and bill payments.

**How are we feeling** – mainly awesome. There have been times where we've had to restrict ourselves from certain things, but can compensate at home (eating at home, watching Netflix, camping inside). But we had a few breakdowns (myself included): frugal living is an every day, every purchase choice and sometimes you don't want to play. But when 1 June 2017 comes around, we can look forward to it.

**A quote I created** – 'A woman with confidence is strong, but a woman with confidence and wealth is unstoppable.' I will be unstoppable for what I believe in, and I want to be in a place where I can give generously and live comfortably within my means.

Thank you for this challenge, Canna; please continue to be unstoppable.

*Tanya*

---

I truly hope that reading these stories from everyday people inspires you – inspires you to have a go, inspires you to see what you're capable of achieving, inspires you to change your future, and most importantly, inspires you to make a better, liberating financial future for yourself. The moment you start to have a go, you will get a little inkling of the incredible power that exists within you. And each time you tap into it, just like exercising a muscle, that power gets stronger and more finely tuned.

You have everything that you need already; now is your turn to pick up those tools and use them. And I promise you, if you embark on the $1000 Project, you will never look back with regret. Life is about to get really exciting for you, with a new awareness and financial mindfulness.

## CHAPTER ELEVEN

# *Sustaining Success*

I wrote this book hoping that by the time you got to this last chapter, you'd be bursting with excitement, motivation and serious insight into what you're capable of achieving.

Now is your time to step up and start your own version of the $1000 Project, designed for and created by you. You'll get to enjoy all the financial, as well as emotional, benefits that come with this personal challenge. And the benefits kick in fast – I bet that the moment you decide to commit to your project, you'll immediately feel a little boost of happiness, an increased sense of direction and even an element of purpose.

One of the things I love about the $1000 Project is that it can come and go as you wish – and it can also stay as long as you wish. When you've achieved one of your goals, or simply need a break, you can park the project for a while and only come back to it when you're ready. You can switch it on and off as you come up with new goals, desires and dreams.

And, depending on your rules, your goals and your boundaries, you can have the $1000 Project as part of your life forever! Whenever you need or want to, you can jump back on board and start consciously moving forward and growing again. Maybe you've decided to start the project to help pay off your student debt – a few years later, you could use it to help buy your first home! Then you might use it to prepare for having a family, then for your children's education – followed by early retirement! The $1000 Project can evolve with you and become part of you and your story.

Use the $1000 Project to move through your life, or maybe even leapfrog through parts of it – to get somewhere new, build something different, own something exciting. It puts you in the driving seat of your own life – for life.

Personally, I get so passionate and excited about taking on the challenge that I go full steam ahead with the project, and throw a lot of energy into each parcel of $1000. By the time my deadline is up, and I analyse my success and look at it with pride and joy, I need a bit of respite – kind of like a financial holiday. I'll indulge in some guilt-free avocado on toast at an expensive cafe – or even in a pair of designer shoes, or a new handbag! I definitely don't go nuts and undo all my hard work, but I also don't feel like I have to justify anything to myself.

When you do the challenge, do it in a balanced way, and reward yourself in a balanced manner. You'll gain insight into the ways in which you value money, and why. You'll find that the knowledge, understanding and awareness that the $1000 Project gives you is addictive, especially as you can see your progress so clearly.

# the $1000 Project can evolve with you and become part of you and your story

It can be a weird feeling finishing the project – kind of like coming back from an extended trip away from your home town. It feels great to be home, and to be settling back in, but you miss the excitement of adventure, exploration and discovery. Often so much so that you might find yourself planning your next adventure, repacking your suitcase and booking new flights!

After a month or two off, I'm ready to restart the $1000 Project with fresh new goals and bubbling motivation. I love the downtime, but I really prefer the direction and vision of working towards a goal (and preferably a variety of goals, not just financial ones).

So don't just put this book down as you finish it. Use it to change your life for the better. You have nothing to lose, and so much to gain.

Outline your goals, brainstorm your ideas, remove any negative self-talk or mental blocks, create your rules and boundaries. And set up that dedicated savings account, named either 'The $1000 Project' or after your specific goal – and start today.

No more excuses, no more procrastination. I've written this book for you because I believe in you, and I believe in everyone around you. Energy is contagious and so is success! Through your own progress, no matter how small, you'll inspire others around you – and they'll inspire others, and the $1000 Project will pick up some serious momentum. I invite you to be a part of this movement right now.

# Recommended Reading

### MOTIVATED MONEY – PETER THORNHILL

If you loved the chapter on shares and want to understand more about why this is my favourite type of investment, I highly recommend that you read this book. It is easy to read and, most importantly, easy to understand. Peter cuts straight to the point and uses cold, hard evidence as to why you need to invest in shares if you are serious about creating long-term financial freedom for yourself.

### THE BEST YEAR OF YOUR LIFE – DEBBIE FORD

Ramp up your goal-setting after reading this book! You will learn how to create great goals that you will never forget, lose interest in or put off. You will awaken something magical inside you where you have cleared the desks to allow the space to move on to greatness.

### *HARMONIC WEALTH* – JAMES ARTHUR RAY

One of my favourite books, given to me by my mother. This was a book that really changed the way I looked at my life and empowered me to dare to try to improve it. It covers not just money, but health, relationships, intellectual growth and spirituality. I owe a lot to this book.

### *THINK AND GROW RICH* – NAPOLEON HILL

This is not easy to read, but there is some really powerful information here that you need to feed your brain, spirit and soul. These messages about mindfulness go back over 100 years. There is so much wisdom in this book.

### *THE MILLIONAIRE NEXT DOOR* – THOMAS J. STANLEY

This will get you thinking about who is really a millionaire – and it isn't who you think. Simplicity pays.

### *HOW TO ATTRACT MONEY USING MIND POWER* – JAMES GOI JR

Not for everyone, but if you are open to the spirituality of money and understand metaphysics, you will appreciate this book and simple steps to help change your beliefs, language and perspective for the better.

### *THE RICHEST MAN IN BABYLON* – GEORGE SAMUEL CLASON

Old-school, but a classic. Great to read with children, giving them advice which will help them throughout their lives.

# Acknowledgments

There is no way this book would be in front of you without some key people in my life. I would like to take a moment to share with you these very special people.

My mum and dad – I am so grateful that my parents taught me from a young age to respect money. I watched them, listened to them and was then encouraged to find my own path. Thank you, Mum and Dad, for keeping me dedicated and accountable to my own financial goals, for believing in me and for supporting me in so many different ways. There is no way I would be where I am if it wasn't for seeing your hard work and discipline and the sacrifices that you made for Jamie and me. I hope that I can instil in my children what you have taught me.

Rocco – my son, my cheeky monkey. I know one of our jobs as parents is to add value to our child's world, but from the moment you entered my life, I feel like I have grown up so much. Since becoming your mother, I have a deeper appreciation for the world we live in, and I want to make it a better and happier place for you and your generation. I am so proud of the little man you are growing into and I hope you always remain true to your spirit. It is an honour to be your mother.

Georgie Abay – one of the kindest, most encouraging and supportive friends a girl would wish for. I distinctly remember when my first book deal was turned down, you were standing with me in the Blue Mountains. Holding back the tears, you gave me the biggest hug and reassured me that something better would come from this and immediately started to help look for solutions and new options. You made it clear that giving up was not an option. Not only have you unconditionally supported and inspired me, but you and your family are like a second family to Rocco, Tom and me, and we are so blessed to have your love, kindness and warmth in our lives. Thank you to you, Mark, Belle and Wottie.

Tom – my biggest critic but my loudest and proudest cheerleader. There are millions of Tom Simpsons out there but only one Tom Simpson like you. No one keeps me grounded, growing and grateful like you do. Even with your nine different personalities. You suddenly appeared in my world and I can't imagine you not in it. Life has never been the same and never been better. Together we laugh (with and at each other!) and it is one of the most beautiful things in our relationship. Thank you for inspiring me to reach higher, for being an incredible role model to Rocco and for caring so much about us. You mean so much to us and you, along with your incredible Simpson clan, make us feel like a team. #unitedfront.

Emily Trinh and Kate Vickery – two amazing girls who have both supported me in different ways. Emily, you have stepped up in the office and shown incredible initiative, efficiency and genuine care. From helping me keep on top of workload and deadlines to supporting me when I have questioned myself, my direction and my strength. Your gentleness, feminine approach and authentic energy is so special and so rare, never forget that. Thank you for everything that you do. Kate, you have always been there for me, listened endlessly to my worries but always shined light on them with your wisdom, insight, maturity and awareness. You know how to help me when I am struggling to figure things out myself and again, I would be lost without you. Thank you.

Peter Thornhill – your passion, enthusiasm and energy has captivated and inspired me since the day I saw you speak at an event in my early twenties. I have since seen you speak many more times, and read your book over and over again, and you never fail to reignite my appreciation for caring about not only my own financial health but also the importance of giving back. So thank you.

Cate Blake – my editor at Penguin Random House. When you offered me this book deal I was terrified. I thought I would fail, be laughed at and have egg on my face. I struggled at school, I am dyslexic and my Microsoft documents have so many red underlines they look like a crime scene. How could I possibly write a book? Each week I submitted a new chapter and you were always so enthusiastic. I thought you were just being polite, but I slowly realised that you genuinely believed in me and my message, and your positive encouragement inspired me to keep going. Thank you for your faith in me, and for the opportunity to get this book out into the world.

My subscribers – the people who have followed me, supported me, shared my message and even given me advice and recommendations. I love creating videos and content for you, and there is no way I would be here today if it wasn't for your kind words, support and engagement. Since starting my channel, my world has massively changed and I hope that I can help create more positive change for you and your family in your own financial future and lifestyle. I genuinely believe in you, the change, growth and improvement that you can make. Thank you for your support and for sharing your stories with me.

xCC